Focus on U.S. History:

The Era of Exploration and Discovery

Kathy Sammis

J. WESTON
WALCH
PUBLISHER
Portland, Maine

User's Guide
to
Walch Reproducible Books

As part of our general effort to provide educational materials which are as practical and economical as possible, we have designated this publication a "reproducible book." The designation means that purchase of the book includes purchase of the right to limited reproduction of all pages on which this symbol appears:

Here is the basic Walch policy: We grant to individual purchasers of this book the right to make sufficient copies of reproducible pages for use by all students of a single teacher. This permission is limited to a single teacher, and does not apply to entire schools or school systems, so institutions purchasing the book should pass the permission on to a single teacher. Copying of the book or its parts for resale is prohibited.

Any questions regarding this policy or requests to purchase further reproduction rights should be addressed to:

Permissions Editor
J. Weston Walch, Publisher
321 Valley Street • P. O. Box 658
Portland, Maine 04104-0658

1   2   3   4   5   6   7   8   9   10
ISBN 0-8251-3334-3

CONTENTS

UNIT 3. WESTERN EUROPE ON THE EVE OF EXPLORATION

UNIT 4. THE EARLY EXPLORERS

UNIT 5. SPAIN AND PORTUGAL IN THE AMERICAS

UNIT 6. SOME CONCLUSIONS

TO THE TEACHER

The study of U.S. history needs to go back further than the first European contact with the Americas. U.S. history really begins when the first human beings moved onto the American continents, at least 20,000 years ago, from Siberia. From the Far North, these early people spread throughout North and South America, developing diverse societies shaped by the widely varied physical and natural environments they settled in. Precolonial American societies ranged from subsistence hunter-gatherers to sophisticated, city-dwelling empire builders.

As these societies continued to evolve and change, Europeans finally arrived, led by bold adventurers willing to cross wild, uncharted oceans. These explorers were the products of their own societies, which were teeming with changes that led naturally to overseas exploration. Once Europeans planted themselves in this exciting "New World," they created economic systems that demanded a plentiful source of cheap labor. They found it in the African slave trade, which brought the third major group of people to the newly developing American culture.

The reproducible student activities in this book are designed to draw students into this experience of early exploration and mutual discovery so they develop a rich understanding of how the history of the United States is underpinned by the initial meeting and mixing of peoples from different parts of the world. Many activities in this book are visual, to give students a more immediate feel for important aspects of the Age of Exploration. Other activities use original source documents to make events that happened centuries ago more immediate and accessible to students by sharing the experiences and thoughts of people who shaped and witnessed them.

Organization

The student activity topics are divided into units guided by the National Standards for History. Each unit begins with a Student Background Sheet that gives the most relevant information on that unit's topic. A number of reproducible student activity pages follow, including reading selections from original contemporary sources, and various analytical, interactive, and interdisciplinary activities.

Each unit includes some Extra Challenge activities to provide enrichment for more advanced or adventurous students. Optional time-line activities suggested in the answer key remind students of chronology, while inviting them into wider descriptive and illustrative areas. Maps are provided in several units as needed.

Each unit is preceded by a Teacher Guide that gives an overview of the unit and its objectives, plus specific teaching suggestions for each student activity.

At the back of this book, the section titled Answers, Additional Activities, and Assessments provides answers for the student activities, suggested additional activities, and an assessment vehicle for each unit. The resource section lists fiction and nonfiction books that will enrich students' learning and be helpful to you, plus media/computer research and enrichment resources. The glossary is reproducible for students' use.

Name _____

Date _____

TO THE STUDENT

 After Columbus arrived in the Americas, in 1492, people from three different continents began to mix, mingle, and merge. Each of these continents had its own cultures—languages, peoples, customs, religious beliefs, political and economic systems— and its own plants and animals, too. United States history begins with the meeting of the peoples, cultures, and natural environments of these different continents.

During the 1400's, Europe was changing a lot. New ideas, strong central governments, money from trade, the crusading tradition— many things got Europe stirred up and ready to start exploring. American societies were continuing to develop, as they had since the first humans migrated across from Asia, tens of thousands of years earlier. West and central African societies had become powerful, wealthy, and sophisticated. But they were losing power and influence when Europeans finally reached them and the transatlantic slave trade began.

The Age of Exploration covers the years when Europeans were finally discovering that the Americas existed. The explorers were spurred by the desire to find sea routes for trade with the Far East, which was very profitable. Many nations explored, but Spain took the lead in becoming a colonial power in the Americas.

The activities you'll be doing for this course of study will help you better understand this era of exploration and mutual discovery. You'll work with maps and graphs. You'll put yourself in the shoes of explorers and colonizers, advising conquistadors and thinking about joining a fabulous caravan across the Sahara. You'll read what explorers had to say about their discoveries and experiences. You'll learn about the houses, daily life, and customs of people in the Americas and Africa before Europeans arrived. You'll find out how Columbus and other explorers were able to cross the unknown ocean to get to the Americas. At the end, you'll have a better grasp of how three continents finally came together, once Columbus arrived, and what some possible results of that contact would be.

The Americas and Early Americans

This unit has two principal objectives: first, to introduce students to the North American physical environment, which has played a significant role in U.S. history; and second, to introduce students to significant aspects of the diverse cultures and peoples of precolonial North America. (We look at Indian peoples of Central and South America in Unit 5.) At first, the Americas had no people. Then, 20,000 or more years ago, peoples began to cross the Bering land bridge into present-day Alaska and spread from there all across both continents, down to South America's southernmost tip. Across the vastness of two continents, these new "native" Americans encountered many different environments and living conditions. Shaped by these diverse lands, the people developed many different societies: nomadic hunter-gatherers, settled agriculturalists, apartment dwellers, and others. Nevertheless, Native American societies shared such common elements as religious beliefs, family structure, and gender roles. Like any other culture, Native American life was continuing to evolve and change when the Europeans finally arrived on the continents. The activities for this unit are designed to draw students into a better understanding of North America and early Americans.

Student Activities

Early Migrations and Peoples presents the early migrations visually, with students drawing the migration waves on their map of North and South America (page 5). They also locate ancient American sites that archaeologists have found on both continents. The Extra Challenge activity allows students to investigate one of those sites in depth and present their findings to the class.

The Map: North America's Environmental Areas shows students the 10 major environmental regions of the continent. Adapting to the particular environment of a region heavily influenced how the Native Americans who inhabited it lived. **Filling Out the Map** draws students into the map by having them add major physical features, then write in the names of representative Native American peoples in the appropriate regions.

A Variety of Dwellings shows students, again, how various Native American peoples adapted to their environment—in this case, via their dwellings.

A Native American Village uses a picture of a Native American village to illustrate life in Indian society. The picture shows a watercolor by Englishman John White, an early colonist.

The All-Purpose Animal demonstrates how thoroughly Plains Indians used their staple of life, the buffalo, by having students identify uses for many labeled parts of the animal.

Speaking in Signs emphasizes that Native Americans spoke a bewildering variety of languages and overcame potential hurdles to communication by developing a widely understood, universal sign language.

Peoples and Places is a four-page chart based on the ten environmental areas of North America. Students fill in the chart, identifying major characteristics of Native American life within each region: geography/climate, sustenance, shelter, social structure/government, major groups/peoples, and typical handicrafts. When the charts are complete, students have a snapshot of the differences and similarities among major groups of Native Americans, and they can more easily analyze the influences of environment and geography on how people lived. (This is a good group activity—see the Answer Key.)

Digging Up the Past makes students aware of how much of our knowledge of early Native American societies comes from archaeology.

Describing Native Americans presents two pages of descriptions of Native Americans written by Europeans who made early contact with them.

Native American Cultures leads students to identify common aspects of Indian culture described by the European writers. In the Extra Challenge activity, students test the validity of what they have just done by investigating a single Native American group and finding common cultural traits in that group's way of life.

An Indian Grant of Land challenges students to evaluate a typical Indian grant of land to Europeans.

Name _____

Date _____

The Americas and Early Americans

At first, tens of thousands of years ago, no human beings lived on the North or South American continents. Then the world experienced several Ice Ages. The most recent one began 30,000 years ago and ended 14,000 years ago. So much water became ice that the sea level fell. A land bridge—the former sea bottom—called ***Beringia*** appeared. Scientists believe this was when the first human beings crossed over from Asia to the American continents. (Some scientists think people may have crossed over during the first Ice Age—50,000 to 40,000 years ago—or even earlier, when Asia and North America were connected—75,000 to 45,000 years ago.)

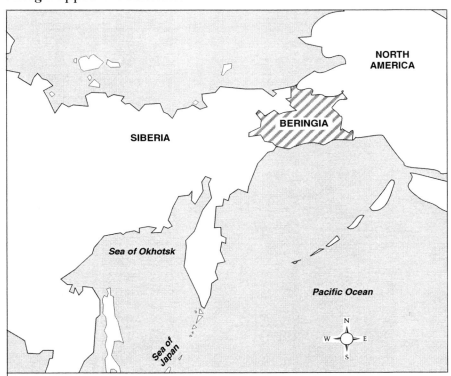

These primitive people spread all over North and South America. They were the ancestors of the American Indians, or Native Americans. They developed many diverse cultures and hundreds of different languages. All lived in close harmony with nature. Their lives were shaped by the special features of the land they lived on, which varied widely across the continents. In this unit, we'll look at the Native American societies of North America.

We'll investigate the societies of South America in Unit 5.

When studying Native American cultures, we can divide the North American continent into **ten environmental regions.** Natural conditions in these regions had a lot to do with how Native Americans who lived there shaped their lives.

(continued)

Focus on U.S. History:
The Era of Exploration and Discovery

The Americas and Early Americans *(continued)*

10 Environmental Regions of North America

Arctic: A frigid region whose people lived in snug domed shelters and hunted.	**Subarctic:** A region with a harsh climate; its people were wandering, or **nomadic**, hunters.	**Northwest Coast:** An area of village-dwelling people with forests rich in fish and game.
Plateau: A harsh, cold area whose people became hunter-gatherers and traders.	**Great Basin:** Cold and snowy; its people were nomads, gathering scarce seasonal resources.	**California:** Small bands of people hunted and gathered in this mild climate.
Southwest: In this semi-desert, people either farmed and lived in apartment houses or hunted and raided.	**Great Plains:** Nomadic buffalo hunting became the way of life on these grasslands.	**Great Forest:** A region of thick forests, rivers, and lakes; its people hunted, fished, farmed, and lived in villages.
	Southeast: In this mild, humid region, village-dwelling people hunted, fished, and farmed.	

While Native American societies were diverse, they did share common elements:

- **Religion** was an important part of everyday life.

- Tribal **authority was shared** among chiefs and elders, who would discuss important issues, then come to a joint decision.

- **Handicrafts** were an important expression of the tribal society.

- **Trade** with other Native American groups was common.

- The society supported itself by **hunting-gathering** and/or by **farming**.

- The people lived in deep **harmony with nature**.

As with all cultures, Native American societies evolved and changed over the years. Monumental changes were to occur when Europeans finally arrived in the Americas.

4

Focus on U.S. History:
The Era of Exploration and Discovery

Name _____

Date _____

Map: North and South America

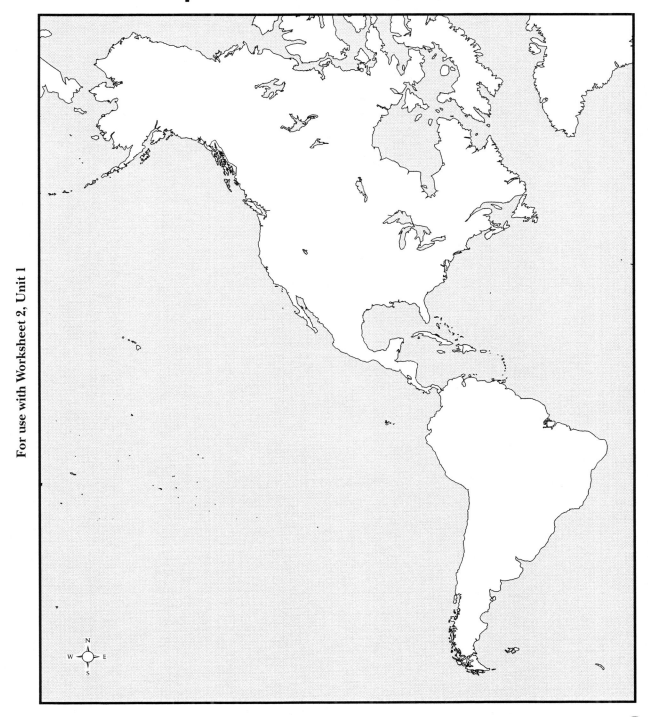

For use with Worksheet 2, Unit 1

Early Migrations and Peoples

The first people to live in the Americas **migrated** (moved) to these continents from **Siberia**, which is in Asia.

Directions: Currently, scientists think the earliest Americans migrated here in several different waves. On your map of North and South America, locate the following waves of migration:

First wave: before 15,000 years ago

Athabascan migration: about 9,000 years ago

Aleut migration: about 4,500 years ago

Further Directions: Scientists find out about ancient people in America by discovering sites where these people lived and left traces of themselves behind. On your migration map, locate and label these sites where ancient Americans lived. The figures in parentheses give the approximate age of each site.

Debert, Nova Scotia (about 10,600 years old)	Old Crow River Basin, Yukon (27,000 years old)
Marmes, Washington (13,000 to 9,000 years old)	Folsom, New Mexico (9,000 years old)
Meadowcroft Rock Shelter, Pennsylvania (15,000 years old)	Clovis, New Mexico (10,000 years old)
Fort Rock Cave, Oregon (14,000 years old)	Wilson Butte, Idaho (15,000 years old)
Laguna Beach, California (17,000 years old)	Selby, Colorado (20,000 years old)
Tlapacoya, Mexico (22,000 years old)	Burnham site, Oklahoma (26,000 years old)
Tepexpán, Mexico (12,000 years old)	Pedra Furada Rock Shelter, Brazil (32,000 years old)
Monte Verde, Chile (34,000 to 14,000 years old)	Taima-Taima, Venezuela (14,500 years old)
Tierra del Fuego, Chile (Fell's Cave) (11,000 years old)	Jayamachay Cave, Peru (22,000 years old)

Extra Challenge: Prepare an illustrated oral or written report on one of the sites on your map. Show and describe the site and artifacts scientists have found there.

Focus on U.S. History:
The Era of Exploration and Discovery

Map: North America's Environmental Areas

For use with Worksheet 4, Unit 1

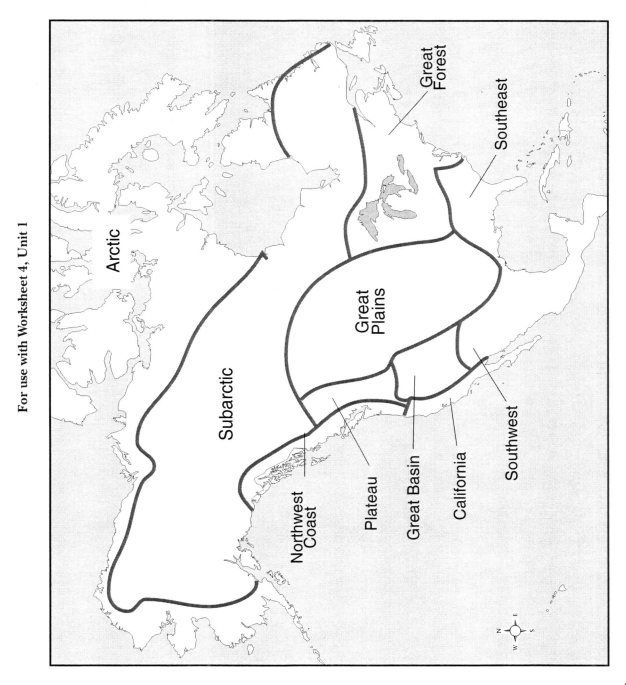

Filling Out the Map

Directions: On your map of the ten environmental areas of North America (page 7), draw in (where needed) and label the physical features listed below. Then add the listed Native American peoples, writing their names in the regions where they lived before the coming of the whites.

Physical Features

Pacific Ocean

Gulf of Mexico

Atlantic Ocean

Hudson Bay

Great Lakes

Rocky Mountains

Appalachian Mountains

Mississippi River

Missouri River

Native American Peoples

Abenaki	Kiowa
Aleut	Klamath
Algonquin	Kwakiutl
Apache	Mandan
Arapaho	Miami
Blackfoot	Micmac
Cherokee	Mohave
Cheyenne	Natchez
Chickasaw	Navajo
Chinook	Nez Percé
Choctaw	Osage
Comanche	Pawnee
Cree	Penobscot
Creek	Powhatan
Crow	Pueblo
Dakota	Seminole
Delaware	Shawnee
Erie	Shoshone
Fox	Susquehannock
Gros Ventre	Tlingit
Haida	Wampanoag
Hopi	Wichita
Huron	Winnebago
Iroquois	Zuni

Focus on U.S. History:
The Era of Exploration and Discovery

A Variety of Dwellings

You might think of a tepee when you think of Native Americans' homes. But early North American peoples built many different types of dwellings for themselves. How and where they lived had a lot to do with the style of their houses.

Extra Challenge: Explain why these people, in this region, might have chosen to build and live in this type of dwelling.

Directions: For each house pictured, tell which Native American people lived in it, in which region of North America, and what the building materials were.

Longhouse

People who lived here: _____

Region where found: _____

Building materials: _____

Reason: _____

People who lived here: _____

Region where found: _____

Building materials: _____

Reason: _____

Adobe buildings

Domed snow house

People who lived here: _____

Region where found: _____

Building materials: _____

Reason: _____

People who lived here: _____

Region where found: _____

Building materials: _____

Chickee

(continued)

Focus on U.S. History:
The Era of Exploration and Discovery

A Variety of Dwellings *(continued)*

Tepee

People who lived here: _____

Region where found: _____

Building materials: _____

Reason: _____

People who lived here: _____

Region where found: _____

Building materials: _____

Reason: _____

Earth lodge

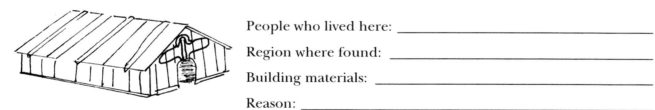

**Rectangular
wooden plank house**

People who lived here: _____

Region where found: _____

Building materials: _____

Reason: _____

People who lived here: _____

Region where found: _____

Building materials: _____

Reason: _____

Domed wigwam

*Focus on U.S. History:
The Era of Exploration and Discovery*

A Native American Village

This drawing, done in 1590, shows daily life in an Indian village located on the Pamlico River, in what is now North Carolina.

Directions: Match each listed item with the letter of the correct area in the picture below.

_____ Cornfield

_____ Dance

_____ Cooking fire

_____ Vegetable garden

_____ Fishing spot

_____ Sprouting field

_____ Hut

_____ Live scarecrow

_____ Hunt

_____ Ceremonial fire

_____ Tobacco fields

_____ Feast

The New York Public Library, *Town of Secotan*, De Bry engraving of John White's watercolor, 1590

11

Focus on U.S. History:
The Era of Exploration and Discovery

Name _____

Date _____

The All-Purpose Animal

After the Plains Indians acquired horses, **buffalo** become the focus of their lives. Peoples such as the Cheyenne and the Sioux became skilled and very successful buffalo hunters. The animals provided many of the necessities of life for Plains dwellers. Little or nothing of a slain buffalo went to waste.

Directions: Write in each box what use Plains Indians made of each buffalo part.

Brain:

Horns:

Hide/skin:

Bones:

Blood:

Meat:

Liver:

Hair:

Intestine:

Teeth:

Buffalo   (*Bison americanus*)

Tail:

Tongue:

Stomach:

Bladder:

Tendons:

Sinew:

Hooves:

Dung:

Focus on U.S. History:
The Era of Exploration and Discovery

Speaking in Signs

Native Americans spoke many different languages. One group could not understand another's spoken words. So, Native Americans developed a widely understood sign language. Here are some sample signs. Practice making them.

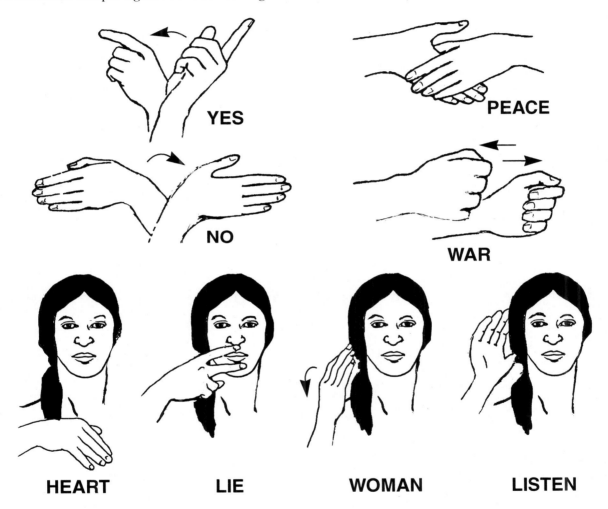

YES

PEACE

NO

WAR

HEART   LIE   WOMAN   LISTEN

Directions: As part of a small group, develop some more signs that you think would be easily understood. Then, using your signs and those above, try to have a conversation with another class group, who will communicate to you in *their* combination of signs. How successful are you in "talking" to one another?

*Focus on U.S. History:
The Era of Exploration and Discovery*

Peoples and Places

Directions: Look at your map of ten North American environmental areas (page 7) and the major geographical features you added to it. Use that information, and other reading you've done, to fill in this four-page chart.

Chart 1

Area	Geography/Climate	Type of Sustenance	Shelter
Arctic			
Subarctic			
Northwest Coast			
Plateau			
Great Basin			

(continued)

Focus on U.S. History:
The Era of Exploration and Discovery

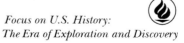

People and Places *(continued)*

When you're finished, you'll have a chart that gives a snapshot of the differences and similarities among major groups of Native Americans. Can you see how their environment and geography affect the way a people live?

Chart 2

Area	Social Structure/ Government	Major Tribal Groups/Peoples	Typical Handicrafts
Arctic			
Subarctic			
Northwest Coast			
Plateau			
Great Basin			

(continued)

Focus on U.S. History:
The Era of Exploration and Discovery

Name _____

Date _____

People and Places *(continued)*

Chart 3

Area	Geography/ Climate	Type of Sustenance	Shelter
California			
Southwest			
Great Plains			
Great Forest			
Southeast			

(continued)

16

Focus on U.S. History:
The Era of Exploration and Discovery

Peoples and Places *(continued)*

Chart 4

Area	Social Structure/Government	Major Tribal Groups/Peoples	Typical Handicrafts
California			
Southwest			
Great Plains			
Great Forest			
Southeast			

Focus on U.S. History:
The Era of Exploration and Discovery

Digging Up the Past

Early Native American societies didn't leave a written record of their lives. So, some of what we know about them comes from *archaeology*—the science of digging up remains of the past in the ground. Archaeologists dig through different *strata*, or layers, of the earth. The deeper the layer, the older the objects found in that layer. Strata from only a few eras are shown here, because of space limits.

Directions: Be an archaeologist! Place each of the objects pictured below in the earliest dated stratum (layer) where it is found.

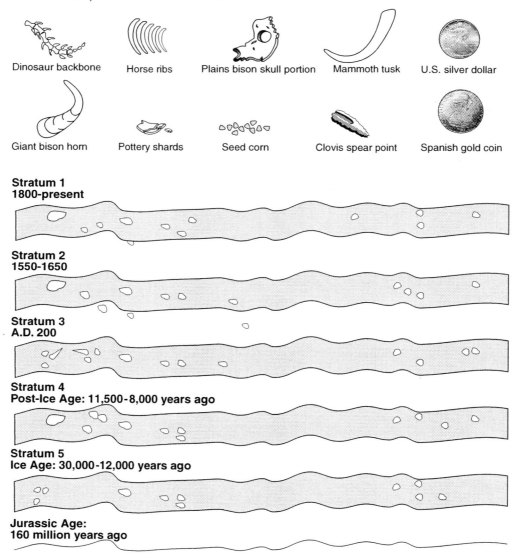

Dinosaur backbone   Horse ribs   Plains bison skull portion   Mammoth tusk   U.S. silver dollar

Giant bison horn   Pottery shards   Seed corn   Clovis spear point   Spanish gold coin

Stratum 1
1800–present

Stratum 2
1550–1650

Stratum 3
A.D. 200

Stratum 4
Post-Ice Age: 11,500–8,000 years ago

Stratum 5
Ice Age: 30,000–12,000 years ago

Jurassic Age:
160 million years ago

Describing Native Americans

Europeans had never met people like Native Americans before. White men who made early contact were eager to describe these new people to the folks back home. Read these descriptions. You'll use these readings in the next activity.

Reverend John Megapolensis (1644) [on the Iroquois]

The government among them consists of the oldest, the most sensible, the best-speaking and most warlike men. These commonly resolve, and the young and warlike men carry into execution. But if the common people do not approve of the resolution, it is left entirely to the judgment of the mob.

The Indians in this country are of much the same stature with us Dutchmen; some of them have very good features, and their bodies and limbs are well proportioned; they all have black eyes, but their skin is tawny. Their hair is very black.

The women are obliged to prepare the land, to mow, to plant, and do everything; the men do nothing except hunting, fishing, and going to war against their enemies.

But although they are so cruel, and have no laws or punishments, yet there are not half so many villainies or murders committed amongst them as amongst Christians. . . . These Indians, though they live without laws, or fear of punishment, do not kill people,
unless they are in a great passion, or fighting.

Thomas Lechford, lawyer (1642) [of the New England Indians]

They are of body tall, proper, and straight. . . . They are naturally proud, and idle, given much to singing, dancing, and plays. . . . Their women are of comely feature, industrious, and do most of the labor in planting, and carrying of burdens. . . . They are of complexion swarthy and tawny. They have all black hair, that I saw.

They live upon parched corn, venison, beavers, otters, oysters, clams, lobsters, and other fish, groundnuts, and acorns. They boil all together in a kettle. Their riches are their wampum, trays, kettles, and spoons, beaver, furs, and canoes. . . . They will give the best entertainment they can make to any English coming amongst them.

They worship Kitan, their good god, or Hobbamocco, their evil god. But they more fear Hobbamocco, because he does them most harm.

(continued)

Describing Native Americans *(continued)*

James Adair, Indian trader (1775)

Most of the Indians have clean, neat dwelling houses, whitewashed within and without, either with decayed oyster shells, coarse chalk, or white marly clay. One or other of [these], each of our Indian nations abounds with, be they ever so far distant from the seashore.

While the Indians were simple in manners, and uncorrupt in morals [before white settlers came], the [white] traders could not be reckoned unhappy; for they were kindly treated, and watchfully guarded, by a society of friendly and sagacious people. . . . Through all the Indian countries, every person lives at his own choice, not being forced in the least degree to any thing contrary to his own inclination.

Captain Jonathan Carver (1767) [of the Northwest tribes]

In their public characters, as forming part of a community, they possess an attachment for that band to which they belong, unknown to the inhabitants of any other country. . . . The honor of their tribe, and the welfare of their nation, is the first and most predominant emotion of their hearts.

They consult without unnecessary opposition, or without giving way to the excitements of envy or ambition. . . . No selfish views ever influence their advice, or obstruct their consultations. Nor is it in the power of bribes or threats to diminish the love they bear their country.

William Strachey, secretary and recorder of Virginia Colony (1618)

They eat, sleep, and dress their meat all under one roof, and in one chamber. . . . About their houses they have commonly square plots of cleared ground, which serve them for gardens.

The men bestow their times in fishing, hunting, wars, and such manlike exercises, outdoors, scorning to be seen in any effeminate labor.

All things they conceive able to do them hurt beyond their prevention, they adore with their kind of divine worship, [such] as the fire, water, lightning, thunder, etc.

Captain Arthur Barlowe, adventurer in Virginia (1584) [of the Roanoke Islanders]

We were entertained with all love and kindness, and with as much bounty (after their manner) as they could possibly devise. We found the people most gentle, loving, and faithful, void of all guile and treason, and such as live after the manner of the golden age. The people only care how to defend themselves from the cold in their short winter, and to feed themselves with such meat as the soil affords.

Focus on U.S. History:
The Era of Exploration and Discovery

Native American Culture

Directions: Native Americans didn't have a single culture. Hundreds of distinct tribal groups lived all over North America. Still, Native Americans shared some common **cultural traits**. From what you've just read, write a brief general description of each of these aspects of Native American culture.

1. Religious beliefs and practices: _____

_____

_____

2. How the community is organized and governed: _____

_____

_____

3. Food sources and types: _____

_____

_____

4. Role of trade and handicrafts: _____

_____

_____

5. Gender roles: _____

_____

_____

6. Social and physical characteristics: _____

_____

_____

Extra Challenge: Choose a specific Native American group. Identify specific aspects of that group's way of life that are examples of the cultural traits you described above.

An Indian Grant of Land

As whites arrived in Indian lands, they often "bought" the land from the Native Americans who lived there. Read this typical grant of land in New Hampshire.

> KNOW ALL MEN BY THESE PRESENTS, that I, Wehanownowit, Sagamore of Piscatoquake, for good considerations . . . which I have received, have granted and sold unto John Wheelwright [and others] all of the right, title, and interest in all such lands, woods, meadows, rivers, brooks, and springs, as of right belong unto me, from the Merrimack River to the patents of Piscatoquake [boundaries are given here]:
>
> TO HAVE AND TO HOLD the same to them and their heirs forever; only the ground which is broken up is excepted, and that it shall be lawful for the said Sagamore to hunt and fish and fowl in the said limits.
>
> IN WITNESS WHEREOF, I have hereunto set my hand the 3d day of April 1638.
>
> Wehanownowit   his mrke

Directions: Think about these questions. Discuss them in a small group, or as a class. Or, you can write an essay answering them.

1. Does this seem like a reasonable treaty, or land grant, to you? What do you find reasonable about it? Unreasonable?

2. Many treaties like this were written and signed between whites and Native Americans. Yet the treaties broke down. Conflicts continued between the two groups of people. Why would this have happened?

Focus on U.S. History:
The Era of Exploration and Discovery

African Roots

The objective of this unit is for students to understand the fullness and complexity of West and central African societies in the period of early contact with Europeans. Approximately 10 to 12 million Africans were forcibly relocated to the Americas during the slave trade. They brought elements of their rich and diverse native cultures to the melting pot that became the new American society. As with Native Americans, West and central Africans were many different peoples speaking many languages, all shaped by their different natural environments. Still, these cultures had some common aspects—in family and group organization, in religious beliefs, and in economic systems. During the 1400's, the great kingdoms of West and central Africa were powerful and extremely wealthy. Their large cities were flourishing centers of trade, scholarship, and court life—and virtually unknown to Europeans. By the time that whites arrived on Africa's west coast, however, the great kingdoms of the Sudan were either mostly gone or in decline. What the whites found, instead, was an opportunity for profitable trade—in slaves. This unit's activity sheets give students a greater understanding of the African-American background.

Student Activities

Mapping Peoples and Places introduces students to the relative locations of empires/kingdoms, towns/cities, and peoples of West and central Africa. Students should use their copies of the reproducible map on page 28.

Mapping African Trade helps students understand African trade, its routes and its items of commerce. Trade was extensive in this part of Africa, a source of great wealth to African empires, yet Europeans had little knowledge of it. The Extra Challenge activity asks students to add trade routes and trade items for East Africa to their map.

The West African Land examines the geography of this part of Africa, which influenced trade and lifestyles. Students identify, then map, the four major climates of the area and complete their maps by locating major physical features.

Two Kinds of Religion helps students identify elements of Islam, which spread to West Africa during the tenth century, in contrast with traditional African religious beliefs. Many African peoples blended the two.

Men's Work, Women's Work presents typical village tasks and asks students to identify gender roles for each one. This provides information for students to compare gender roles in African and Native American societies on the Unit 3 chart, "Three Worlds About to Meet."

The African-American Food Swap demonstrates to students that contact between Europeans and Africans during the shipment of slaves to the Americas wasn't all one way. By identifying the movement of various foods from one continent to another, students learn that even the least equitable contact between two peoples is bound to result in two-way exchanges of some sort. **The Columbian Exchange** in Unit 6 extends this activity to mutual exchanges among Europeans, Africans, and Native Americans.

Cities of the African Empires presents contemporary descriptions of Africa's medieval empires at their height. The directed comparison with a European city of the same era underscores for students how sophisticated and complex West African cities were. You may want to suggest appropriate European cities for comparison; otherwise, students can choose their own.

African Buildings is similar to the Unit 1 activity **A Variety of Dwellings**. Students identify materials and reasons for design of three typical West African dwellings. The Extra Challenge activity asks students to identify a picture taken from a contemporary drawing of an African city—it's Timbuktu—and note the mix of traditional African and Arab/Islamic building design, which is mentioned in the **Close-up**. (If you haven't done the **Close-up** yet, tell students they'll find the answer to the building design question when they read that page.)

Close-up: Mansa Musa's Fabulous Journey tells the story of how a Mali ruler's *hajj*, or pilgrimage to Mecca, in the 1320's caused the Cairo gold market to crash. The worksheet includes suggestions for various activities related to Mansa Musa for students to complete.

African Roots

The North American continent was first populated tens of thousands of years ago by **migrants** from Asia, as you learned in Unit 1. In modern times, European explorers and settlers arrived. You'll read about them in later units of this book. The third major population group to come to the Americas was black Africans. Almost all of them came against their will, as slaves.

As American slaves, blacks—mostly from West and central Africa—were forced into a new and unfamiliar culture. But they brought with them elements of their rich and diverse native cultures. Because of African geography, these cultures were largely unknown to Europeans. The vast Sahara Desert separated North Africa from the rest of the continent. Arab traders, African slaves, and Muslim travelers crossed the desert in camel caravans. Europeans did not. If they had, they would have been amazed at what they found: well-ordered political empires, busy trading networks, and cities full of merchants, scholars, and artisans.

West Africa is a vast area, with different types of **terrain** (ground) and many diverse peoples. The terrain can be broken up into belts, or layers:

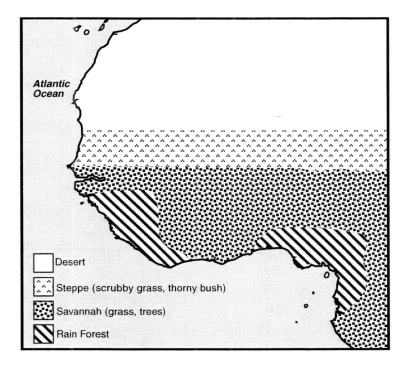

Atlantic Ocean

☐ Desert

▵ Steppe (scrubby grass, thorny bush)

▪ Savannah (grass, trees)

╱ Rain Forest

(continued)

African Roots (continued)

The people of this area were of many different **ethnic, tribal, and language groups**. But they shared certain characteristics. About 2,000 years ago, they learned how to make tools and weapons out of iron. Farming and hunting became much easier and more successful. Populations and villages grew. They were held together by a strong social fabric based on kinship, or common ancestry. Group harmony and welfare were the highest values. Spiritual life was not separate from physical life. The community included dead ancestors and generations not yet born. West African artwork expresses these close ties to the spiritual and natural worlds.

Along with these simple village societies, great cities and empires grew in West Africa. They gained wealth and power from their vast stores of **gold**. Among them were:

Ghana: Rose around A.D. 700, fell around 1200.	**Mali:** Emerged around A.D. 1200, fell around 1500. Much larger than Ghana.	**Songhay:** A.D. 1350–1600. Farther east than Mali. Destroyed by invaders from Morocco.

The cities of these empires were impressive centers of trade, learning, and court life. Timbuktu, the major city of Mali, had so many scholars that books were a major item of its trade. **Trade caravans** came south to the cities with salt and European goods from North Africa. Traders exchanged these for gold, slaves, kola nuts, and ivory.

The West African empires and smaller kingdoms were mostly ruled by "divine" kings, or chiefs. These kings were godlike, with close ties to the spirit world. Actual governing was done by the king's counselors, or by local kings and heads of provinces. Power was held along clan lines. In non-kingdom areas, the **village** was the basic unit, governed mostly by democracy.

City life and **village life** in West Africa were quite different. Here are some common professions in each:

City	Village
Merchant	Fisherman
Soldier	Livestock tender
Scholar	Crop grower
Cleric	Basket maker
Doctor	Priestess
King's servant	Hunter

Most traditional African religions believed in one supreme God. This **deity** played no direct role in human affairs. All sorts of lesser gods directed the physical workings of the world; prayers and ceremonies were directed to these spirits. Ancestors, too, were called on to help win the gods' favor. **Sorcery** and witchcraft—good magic and bad magic—were also very much a part of African spiritual life.

(continued)

*Focus on U.S. History:
The Era of Exploration and Discovery*

African Roots *(continued)*

Islam spread to West Africa during the tenth century. With it came literacy, the use of currency and credit, and law codes. Many Africans accepted Islam's belief in a single supreme God and adopted Islamic rituals. In many cases, they also held on to their native beliefs in lesser gods and spirits.

These, then, were the societies from which black American slaves were taken. When Europeans finally arrived along the coast of Africa in the fifteenth century, the great empires of the Sudan were gone or in decline. (Benin and Oyo, though, were still flourishing.) The Europeans traded along the coast. Local rulers produced trade goods—mostly slaves—from the interior. Exchanges took place at coastal trading forts. European traders remained ignorant about all aspects of African culture—political, religious, social, artistic. Africans carried to America in slavery, however, remembered their roots and planted them in the New World.

African and American Slavery

Slavery was an ancient part of African society. People became slaves when they were captured as prisoners of war, as punishment for a crime, or to pay off a debt. African rulers often sold slaves to one another, and they had been selling slaves to Arab traders for centuries. When Europeans arrived in Africa, they discovered this slave trade. Plantations in America soon needed vast numbers of laborers. The African-American slave trade began and expanded rapidly.

There was a big difference between African and American slavery. African slaves became part of a family group. They could advance to freedom through marriage or by self-purchase. Slaves in the Americas, however, were almost always enslaved for life. Their children, too, were slaves.

Name _____

Date _____

Map: West and Central Africa

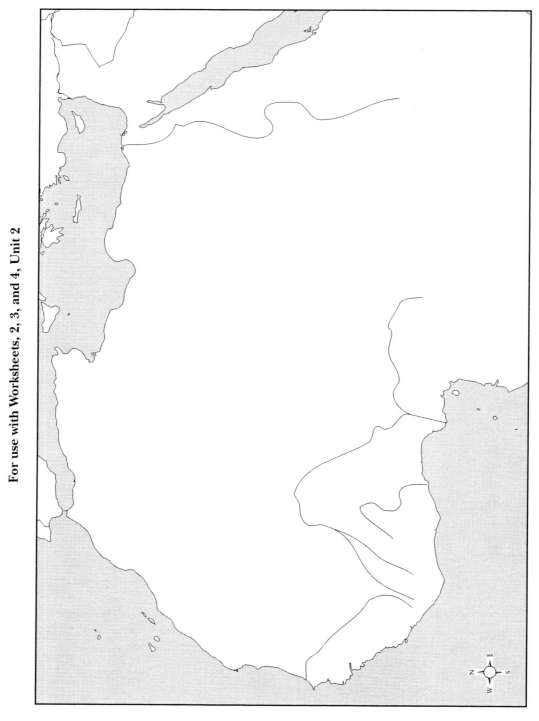

For use with Worksheets, 2, 3, and 4, Unit 2

Focus on U.S. History:
The Era of Exploration and Discovery

Mapping Peoples and Places

Directions: On your map of West and Central Africa, locate and label the following empires/kingdoms, towns/cities, and areas where the listed peoples lived. Circle the names of empires, kingdoms, and peoples on your map.

Cities/Towns		Empires/Kingdoms
Timbuktu	Ife	GHANA
Gao	Benin	MALI
Jenne	Elmina	SONGHAY
Takedda	Axim	BENIN
Taghaza	Kano	OYO
Koumbi Saleh	Niani	**Peoples**
Bilma	Tadmekka	Soninke
Walata	Awdoghast	Songhay
		Tuareg
		Mossi
North African Trading Centers		Fulani
Ghadames	Marrakech	Malinke
Algiers	Sijilmasa	Arab
Tangier	Fez	Berber
Alexandria	Tunis	Yoruba
Cairo	Tripoli	Bini

Mapping African Trade

Directions: West Africa was a hub of trading activity. On your map of West and Central Africa, draw the following trade routes. On the map, write items that were traded in the regions where they originated.

Routes	Trade items
From Tangier, Fez, and Marrakech	Gold
From Algiers	Salt
From Tunis	Copper
From Tripoli	Books
Among West African cities/towns	Manufactured items
To the southern Atlantic coast	Horses
	Slaves
	Kola nuts
	Metalware
	Melegueta pepper
	Luxury goods

Extra Challenge: To the complete map of Africa in Unit 4, add the trade routes and trade items for Africa's east coast and southern interior.

Focus on U.S. History:
The Era of Exploration and Discovery

Name _____

Date _____

The West African Land

Directions—Part 1: West and central Africa have many different physical features and climates. Match each description below with the correct name for that region.

1. Hot temperatures, heavy annual rainfall, high humidity, dense tree growth:

   _____

2. Tropical; light and variable annual rainfall; sometimes long droughts; scrubby grasslands and thorny bush:

   _____

3. Very little rainfall; wide temperature differences between day and night; almost no vegetation:

   _____

4. Tropical wet-dry; long dry season and a short, wet summer; grasslands and trees:

   _____

Savannah

Desert (Sahara)

Tropical rain forest

Tropical steppe (Sahel)

Directions—Part 2: Now, show on your map of Africa where each region you named in Part 1 is found. Also, locate and label these other physical features on the map.

Rivers	Mountains	*Coasts
Gambia	Fouta Djallon	Ivory Coast
Senegal	Aïr	Gold Coast
Niger		Slave Coast
Nile	**Bodies of Water**	Pepper Coast
Bani	Atlantic Ocean	
Black Volta	Mediterranean Sea	**Capes**
White Volta	Bight of Benin	Bojador
Benue	Lake Chad	Verde
		Blanc
Desert		
Sahara		

* Names used by European traders

Focus on U.S. History:
The Era of Exploration and Discovery

Two Kinds of Religion

Islam is the Muslim religion, founded by Muhammad in A.D. 610. It spread to West Africa during the tenth century. Some Africans adopted Islam. Some kept to their traditional religious beliefs and practices. Others blended the two religions.

Directions: Contrast aspects of Islam and traditional African religions in each area listed below. Write some differences on the lines provided.

Prayer/Religious Buildings

Islam: _____

_____

African: _____

_____

Food/Eating

Islam: _____

_____

African: _____

_____

God(s)

Islam: _____

_____

African: _____

_____

Women's Roles

Islam: _____

_____

African: _____

_____

Slavery

Islam: _____

_____

African: _____

_____

Toleration of Other Religions

Islam: _____

_____

African: _____

_____

Men's Work, Women's Work

Directions: As in most traditional societies, African villages often assigned certain jobs to men and others to women. Some jobs, though, both sexes might perform. For each task below, write *men, women,* or *both* to identify who usually performed this job.

Food production

Planting and tending crops: _____

Harvesting crops: _____

Processing foods: _____

Hunting for meat: _____

Fishing: _____

Making things

Making pots: _____

Making baskets: _____

Weaving: _____

Making tools: _____

Making weapons: _____

Making utensils: _____

Village tasks

Clearing land: _____

Building houses: _____

Tending chickens: _____

Commerce

Marketing surplus crops: _____

Trading other goods: _____

Mining gold: _____

Serving in the military: _____

The African-American Food Swap

Directions: Once trade was established between the Americas and Africa, native foods began to cross the Atlantic. Some became very important in their adopted homelands. Identify below the direction in which each food crop moved from continent to continent. (Draw an arrow from Africa to America, or from America to Africa, whichever is correct.)

America	Food	Africa
	Maize (corn)	
	Yams	
	Peanuts	
	Tomatoes	
	Millet	
	Melegueta pepper	
	Cacao	
	Sorghum	
	Rice	
	Squash varieties	
	Sweet potatoes	
	Okra	
	Bean varieties	

Cities of the African Empires

Life in Africa's medieval empires was rich, orderly, and interesting. Here are some descriptions written by travelers of those times.

al-Bakri (a Spanish Moor who collected travelers' accounts): Ghana in 1067

The king of Ghana can put 200,000 warriors in the field, more than 40,000 being armed with bow and arrow . . . When he gives audience to his people, to listen to their complaints and set them to rights, he sits in a pavilion around which stand his horses . . . in cloth of gold. Behind him stand ten pages holding shields and gold-mounted swords. And on his right are the sons of the princes of his empire, splendidly clad and with gold plaited into their hair. The governor of the city is seated on the ground in front of the king, and all around him are his viziers in the same position. The gate of the chamber is guarded by dogs of an excellent breed, who never leave the king's seat. They wear collars of gold and silver, ornamented with the same metals.

Ibn Battuta (a Moroccan Berber who traveled widely): Mali around 1352

The Negroes are of all people those who most abhor injustice. The sultan pardons no one who is guilty of it. One enjoys complete and general safety throughout the land. The traveler has no more reason than the man who stays at home to fear brigands, thieves or ravishers.

Abderrahman es-Sadi (a native of Timbuktu): Jenne in the 1600's

This city is great, flourishing and prosperous. It is one of the great markets of the Muslim world. Here gather the merchants who bring salt from the mines of Taghaza and those who bring gold from the mines of Bittou. . . . It is because of this fortunate city that the caravans flock to Timbuktu from all points of the horizon.

(continued)

Cities of the African Empires *(continued)*

Leo Africanus (Moorish traveler, Muslim convert to Christianity): Timbuktu around 1512

Here in Timbuktu there are great stores of doctors, judges, priests, and other learned men, well supported at the king's cost and charges. And here are brought many manuscripts or written books from North Africa, which are sold for more money than any other merchandise.

Here are many shops of artificers and merchants, and especially of such as weave linen and cotton cloth. And hither do the North African merchants bring cloth of Europe. All the women of this region except the maid servants go with their faces covered, and sell all necessary victuals. The inhabitants, and especially strangers living there, are exceeding rich . . .

Here are many wells containing most sweet water; and so often as the River Niger overflows, they convey the water of it by sluices into the town. Corn, cattle, milk, and butter this region yields in great abundance. But salt is very scarce here, for it is brought hither by land from Taghaza.

Directions: Compare life in the cities of the African empires with life in European cities at the same time. For each item listed below, choose a European city for comparison.

1. Trade in Jenné in the 1600's / European contrast: _____

   _____

2. The royal court and army in Ghana in 1607 / European contrast: _____

   _____

3. Timbuktu as a learning center in 1512 / European contrast: _____

   _____

4. Commerce in Timbuktu in 1512 and/or in Jenné in the early 1600's / European contrast:

   _____

   _____

5. Water and food supply in Timbuktu in 1512 / European contrast: _____

   _____

Name _____

Date _____

African Buildings

Directions: West Africans used native materials to construct their homes. Arab influences also affected building design in some areas. Identify the building materials and reasons for each design.

1.

Building materials: _____

_____

Reason for design: _____

_____

2.

Building materials: _____

_____

Reason for design: _____

_____

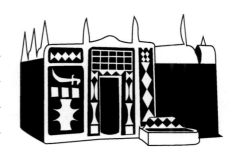

3.

Building materials: _____

_____

Reason for design: _____

_____

4.

Extra Challenge: What do you think this picture might be?

_____

What mix of building designs do you see here? Why?

_____

_____

37

Focus on U.S. History:
The Era of Exploration and Discovery

Close-up: Mansa Musa's Fabulous Journey

Mansa Musa was the ruler of Mali in the 1300's. Like many of his people, he was a devout Muslim. One of the five basic obligations of Islam is to make a *hajj*, a religious pilgrimage, to Mecca and Medina. They are holy cities of Islam in the Middle East.

Mansa Musa set off on his *hajj* in 1324. He was no ordinary pilgrim. Five hundred slaves marched before him. Each one carried a six-pound staff of gold. One hundred camels carried hundreds of pounds of gold each. Many more camels carried the caravan's supplies. Thousands of people came along on the *hajj*.

Mansa Musa stopped for a while in Cairo, Egypt. Then he went on to Arabia and the holy cities. During this trip, people of the Middle East learned that rumors of a fabulously wealthy African kingdom south of the Sahara Desert were true. Mansa Musa paid for everything he purchased—food, clothing, lodgings, merchants' goods of all kinds—in gold. He spent so much gold that its value dropped sharply. The Cairo gold market took years to recover.

As a by-product of the *hajj*, building styles in the Malian area of West Africa changed. Mansa Musa brought a North African Islamic architect back to Mali with him. This man, es-Saheli, introduced flat-topped roofs. He also added protruding wooden posts to house sides that made it easier to repair mud walls.

Directions: Read some more about Mansa Musa's life. Write a biography of him. Or, create an illustration of Mansa Musa's *hajj* caravan. With classmates, you could also present a skit about some aspect of Mansa Musa's life. Or, pretend to be a young servant or slave accompanying Musa on his *hajj;* write a series of diary entries about your experiences.

Focus on U.S. History:
The Era of Exploration and Discovery

Western Europe on the Eve of Exploration

The objective of this unit is for students to understand the characteristics of European society in the 1400's that helped create the Age of Exploration. Trade was a big factor. European demand for eastern goods was high; it made bold thinkers wonder about sea routes to the Far East. In addition, the end of the Crusades and the *reconquista* of Islamic Spain left no outlet for the zeal that many people still felt to conquer "heathen" peoples and spread Christianity. Strong central governments created stable states, capable of supporting voyages of exploration. The growth of commerce and urban centers created wealth to finance such voyages. The Renaissance and the Reformation spurred people to think in new ways and reexamine previously accepted knowledge. People tackled questions of science and geography with a new spirit of empiricism. The Age of Exploration was a natural outgrowth of all of this. This unit's activities draw students into a greater understanding of European society on the eve of the Age of Exploration.

Student Activities

East-West Trade presents the exploration-inducing trade between Europe and the Far East in map form. Students locate important cities and physical features and identify items of trade and their origins. They also draw in the important trade routes, which demonstrate why nations like Spain, Portugal, the Netherlands, and England ultimately sought alternative routes.

Spurs to the Age of Exploration is a small-group activity. Students are given events and developments in Europe in the 1400's and 1500's, and asked to identify how each helped fuel the Age of Exploration. Then they develop a visual presentation of their findings. Groups could tackle just one or two topics rather than all of them, at your discretion.

The Countries of Europe asks students to create capsule portraits of the main European nations that became involved in the Age of Exploration.

Three Worlds About to Meet provides a frame for students to compare the three worlds—European, African, Native American—that were about to meet in the late 1400's and 1500's.

Western Europe on the Eve of Exploration

The All-Important Spices

Why were spices so important? For one thing, they made food tastier. Another more vital reason was that Europeans didn't have much ice (except in northern areas in the winter). Meat spoiled easily—but it was still served, even after it had spoiled. Spices helped preserve meat. They also masked the spoiled taste. Yum!

Western Europe in the 1400's was a lively place. Changes were happening in politics, in the economy, in religion, and in knowledge and thought. **Trade** was very important, especially trade with the East. Europeans wanted eastern luxury goods and, above all, spices. The long trip (overland, or by sea and then land) from the Far East was dangerous and expensive. Italian city-states that controlled this trade, like Venice and Genoa, became very wealthy. Countries like Spain and Portugal wanted a share of the trade. They began to look for other, all-sea routes to the East.

The way people lived in Europe began to change in the 1400's, too. Trade was part of this. It was a kind of chain reaction.

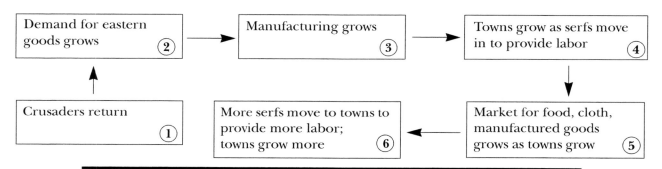

Demand for eastern goods grows ② → Manufacturing grows ③ → Towns grow as serfs move in to provide labor ④

Crusaders return ① ↑

More serfs move to towns to provide more labor; towns grow more ⑥ ← Market for food, cloth, manufactured goods grows as towns grow ⑤

The Legacy of the Crusades

The **Crusades**, which ended just before 1300, had a big influence on Western Europe, too. Armies of European Christians had trooped to the Middle East to try to take back the Holy Lands from the Muslims. When the Crusaders came home, they had developed a strong taste for eastern foods and luxury goods. This demand fueled trade. The Crusaders had also been inflamed with a spirit of adventure, a zeal to spread Christianity to "heathen" people,

and a taste for conquest. Such urges found a natural outlet in the voyages of exploration that were soon to come.

Strong Central Governments

Political systems in Europe changed during the 1400's. The Black Death (plague) of the 1340's had helped to break down feudalism, which strong central governments replaced.

(continued)

Focus on U.S. History:
The Era of Exploration and Discovery

Western Europe on the Eve of Exploration *(continued)*

England
Chaotic Wars of the Roses end as a strong monarch, supported by rich city merchants, takes the throne in 1485.

France
Takes back almost all English lands in France. Two strong kings build royal power.

Portugal
Under Prince Henry the Navigator, the nation focuses on overseas trade and exploration.

Spain
Ferdinand and Isabella marry, uniting two kingdoms into one strong central monarchy; Moorish control ends.

Italy
City-states directed by merchants grow wealthy and powerful through trade.

European countries with strong central governments became stable. Business and trade expanded, and nations became wealthy. They could support fleets of ships and armies. Their national pride was increasing. They began to look across the seas, to where they might increase their power and wealth. They might also find precious metals there—gold and silver—to make into **currency** to pay for their trade.

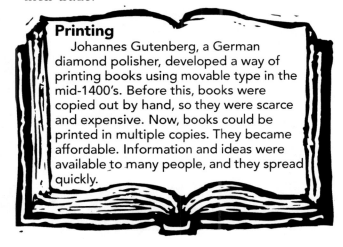

Printing
Johannes Gutenberg, a German diamond polisher, developed a way of printing books using movable type in the mid-1400's. Before this, books were copied out by hand, so they were scarce and expensive. Now, books could be printed in multiple copies. They became affordable. Information and ideas were available to many people, and they spread quickly.

The Renaissance

Another big change was taking place in Europe during the 1400's—the **Renaissance**. This was a major cultural and intellectual movement that changed the way European people thought and looked at the world. Scholars rediscovered the classical texts of Greece and Rome, including Ptolemy's studies of geography. Medieval thinkers had accepted that knowledge was proclaimed by God and spread through Church teachings. But Renaissance thinkers took an individual, fact-based approach to knowledge. People questioned old assumptions and myths, including old geography fables. Individual thoughts and actions became valued. People's imaginations were fired, and they wanted to learn more about themselves, nature, religion, science—the world. Soon, they were to learn that the world was more than they had ever imagined.

Map: Europe, Asia, Africa—Trading Partners

For use with Worksheet 2, Unit 3

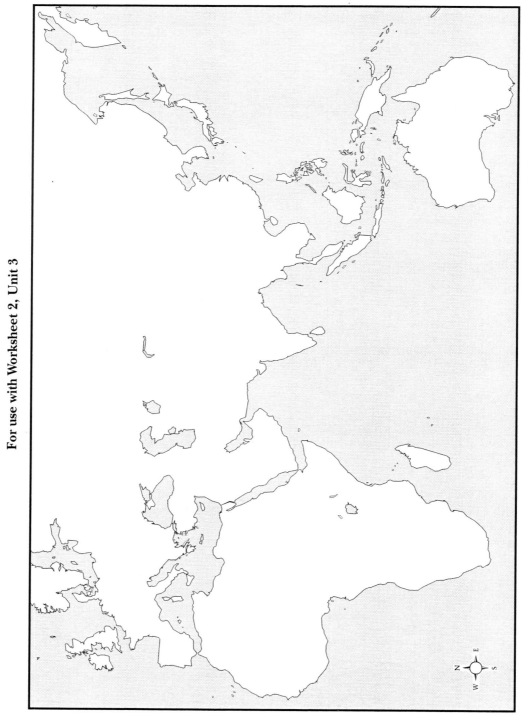

East-West Trade

Demand for eastern goods was high in Europe during and after the Middle Ages. Europeans paid for these goods with African gold.

Directions: On your map of Europe, Asia, and Africa, trace the major trade routes. Also, locate and label the cities and physical features listed below. Then write in the names of the trade goods to show where they came from.

Trade Routes
• Overland from China, then to Europe
• By sea from eastern islands, ultimately to Europe
• By camel caravan from West Africa

Trade Goods		Cities	
Spices	Dyestuffs	Samarkand	Alexandria
Gems	Tea	Antwerp	Damascus
Gold	Coffee	Timbuktu	Genoa
Silk	Slaves	Malacca	London
Manufactured goods	Horses	Calicut	Constantinople
Perfumes	Dates	Hormuz	Tangier
Steel	Carpets	Mecca	Tunis
Woolen cloth	Cotton cloth	Venice	

Bodies of Water		Islands	
Indian Ocean	Mediterranean Sea	Moluccas (Spice Islands)	Indonesia
Pacific Ocean	Black Sea	Ceylon	Japan
Atlantic Ocean	Baltic Sea	Madagascar	
Red Sea		**Desert**	
		Sahara	

43

Focus on U.S. History:
The Era of Exploration and Discovery

Spurs to the Age of Exploration

Directions: Do this activity as part of a small group. The events and developments listed below affected Europe in the 1400's and 1500's. Your task is to:

(a) identify how **each helped fuel** the Age of Exploration, then

(b) develop a **chart** or other **visual presentation** of your findings for class display.

Renaissance

A rebirth of learning and scientific thought, 1400's–1600's

Protestant Reformation

Protestant churches come into existence, breaking off from the Catholic Church, 1500's

---

Strong central governments

Developed in Europe, 1500's

Black Death

Bubonic plague killed huge numbers of people, mid-1300's

Spread of Islam

Muslim rule expanded to Constantinople in 1453

Crusades

European Christians battle Muslims for the Holy Land, 1000's–1200's

---

Reconquista **of Spain**

Spanish Christians drive out Moorish occupiers, 1200's–1400's

---

Printing

Gutenberg develops movable type, 1400's

The Countries of Europe

Directions: Get to know the European countries that were involved in exploration. Fill in the boxes below with each country's religion, language, and form of government.

ENGLAND

Main religion

Main language

Type of government

SPAIN

Main religion

Main language

Type of government

ITALY

Main religion

Main language

Type of government

FRANCE

Main religion

Main language

Type of government

PORTUGAL

Main religion

Main language

Type of government

NETHERLANDS

Main religion

Main language

Type of government

ENGLAND

NETHERLANDS

FRANCE

ITALY

PORTUGAL

SPAIN

Extra Challenge: Report on the somewhat confusing status of the Netherlands from the 1300's through the creation of the Dutch Republic in the 1600's. How did this history affect Dutch participation in the Age of Exploration?

*Focus on U.S. History:
The Era of Exploration and Discovery*

Three Worlds About to Meet

Directions: Three worlds—European, Native American, and African—are about to meet and mingle. From what you have read, fill in these boxes to **compare and contrast** those worlds. (Of course, societies within Europe, within Africa, and within the Americas were diverse. For this activity, identify **broad general characteristics** that applied to many peoples in each area.)

	Europe	Africa	America
Political system			
Social organization			
Economic system			
Main ideas and values			

Focus on U.S. History:
The Era of Exploration and Discovery

The Early Explorers

The objective of this unit is for students to understand the course of European overseas exploration from 1492 to 1700. The Portuguese began the Age of Exploration with their voyages down the coast of Africa, searching for the eastern route to the Spice Islands. Columbus countered by sailing west to arrive at the Indies. While he was not the first European to reach the Americas, his landfall does mark the "discovery" of the American continents. With Columbus's voyages, knowledge of the New World soon became widespread among Europeans, and Americans and Europeans were henceforward inextricably intertwined. This unit's activities draw students into a greater understanding of the years of European exploration.

Student Activities

Voyages of Discovery presents the wide sweep of the Age of Exploration by having students draw the routes of major voyages. The Extra Challenge questions ask students to identify the explorers who sailed for countries other than their own (like Columbus) and to use their math skills to calculate the length of some of the voyages.

The Route East reacquaints students with the geography of Africa. It focuses on stages of Portugal's quest to find the sea route around the continent by having students locate and label landmarks of that quest. The Extra Challenge activities ask students to identify the sea captains involved in the quest and to liven up their maps with drawings of the fearsome dangers sailors expected to encounter as they sailed southward.

Boats, Boats, Boats underscores, visually and in writing, the importance of improvements in boat design to the Age of Exploration. Students are given pictures and names of various sailing ships; they are asked to identify the nation/people who used each one, the waters where it generally sailed, and its advantages and disadvantages.

Navigation Aids shows students the navigational tools that made overseas voyages possible. Students deepen their understanding by identifying each tool and its purpose. The Extra Challenge activity invites students to explain how at least one of these tools actually worked.

Columbus and the "Ocean Sea" shows, in Part 1, the glaring inaccuracies of the world maps that Columbus used to plan his exploratory voyages. Students identify the inaccuracies and explain their effects. Part 2 of this activity uses a map of the prevailing winds and currents of the Atlantic Ocean. By charting courses across the Atlantic, students gain an understanding of how Columbus and the Vikings were able to make their round-trip voyages.

Christopher Columbus: In His Own Words presents two pages of entries from Columbus's daily log of his first voyage in 1492.

The follow-up activity, **What Columbus Tells Us**, has students interpret Columbus's comments to see what they reveal about (1) his intentions and (2) the beginning and subsequent relations between Europeans and native American peoples.

Who Really Discovered America? brings up the question of Columbus's predecessors. Working in small groups, students choose one of six pre-Columbian "discoverers" of America, actual or perhaps only legendary. After researching their discoverer(s), student groups make the case to their classmates that their subject was the first person to reach the Americas after the prehistoric peoples of Asia. After all groups have presented their cases, you could lead a class discussion and hold a vote, to see who students think really did reach America before Columbus.

Why Explore? gives students a frame to compare and contrast the different motives that Portugal, Spain, England, France, and the Netherlands had for exploration. In the Extra Challenge activity, students test the motives they've identified by applying them to a particular explorer or early colonizer.

The Early Explorers

> The Portuguese were right about their all-sea trade route to the Far East being profitable. Vasco da Gama made the first round trip along this route in 1497–99. The sale of the Eastern goods he brought back netted 60 times more than the expedition had cost!

The Portuguese thought they knew, and they were right. Their prince, Henry the Navigator, inspired a series of voyages down the West Coast of Africa. The aim was to find a sea route around the southern tip of Africa. Then Portuguese ships could sail directly to the Far Eastern trade ports. This would make Portugal wealthy and powerful. Bit by bit during the

1400's, adventurous Portuguese sea captains made their way down Africa. Finally, **Bartholomeu Dias** battled his way around Africa's Cape of Good Hope in **1488**. The trade route was open.

Columbus

Christopher Columbus thought he knew where he was going, too. He read books, studied charts, and sailed a lot. He became convinced he could sail west across the "Ocean Sea" to Japan and the Spice Islands—the Indies. (There wasn't supposed to be much ocean between Europe and Asia.) King Ferdinand and Queen Isabella of Spain backed Columbus's voyages. The monarchs and Columbus wanted glory and wealth, and to serve God by spreading Christianity. Columbus did sail west in **1492**, and he did find an area full of beautiful islands. He died thinking that he really had reached the Indies, which is why he called the natives of the region *Indians.*

> "New islands, new lands, new seas, new peoples; and, what is more, a new sky and new stars."—Pedro Nunes, 1537

Nunes's words express the vastness of what the early explorers discovered. To his list we could add "new plants" and "new animals." To make these discoveries, early explorers had to cross huge, rough, uncharted seas. They would arrive—where? No one knew for sure, at first.

Question:

What does Nunes mean by "a new sky and new stars"?

(continued)

The Early Explorers (continued)

The "New World"

Columbus didn't know what he had found, but others figured it out pretty quickly. **Juan de la Cosa**, one of his shipmates, returned to the Caribbean in **1499**. De la Cosa then issued a map that showed, for the first time, the existence of the "New World" lands. **Amerigo Vespucci**, sailing for the Spanish in **1499** and for the Portuguese in **1501**, explored the northern coast of South America. Many people read what he wrote about his voyage. A German mapmaker, Martin Waldeseemüller, labeled his map of the "New World" lands *America*, a Latin version of Vespucci's first name.

Ferdinand Magellan started on the ultimate voyage of exploration in **1519**. He set out to sail around the world. He didn't make it; he was killed in a battle between natives of the Philippines. But one of his ships, the *Victoria*, captained by **Juan Sebastián del Cano**, made it back to Spain in **1522**.

Portugal (in Brazil) and Spain (in Central and South America) soon had very profitable colonies. Other European countries were slow to get into the act. France and England had been upset by religious and political conflicts. But conditions changed later in the 1500's.

Spain's power in Europe started to slip. Rival nations began to challenge her control of the seas. The Protestant Reformation threatened to split the Catholic Church. Merchant classes became powerful in England, France, and the Netherlands, and these countries began to send out explorers, too. English sea captains searched for a northwest passage through the Americas to the Far East. (They failed.) French explorers went inland, sailing and paddling their way along the Great Lakes and rivers like the Saint Lawrence and the Mississippi. The Dutch sent **Henry Hudson** to explore, and soon after set up trading posts in present-day New York.

The **Age of Exploration** introduced the Americas to Europe, and vice versa. But contact between the Americas and other peoples had occurred long before Columbus. The **Vikings** were Norse adventurers. Originally from Norway, they settled in Iceland and then Greenland. From there, they voyaged to "Vinland," which is North America, around 1000.

Others may have come to the Americas, too—Africans, Phoenicians, Celts, Welsh, Pacific islanders. We simply don't know—at least, not yet. But the significant "discovery" was the one that Columbus made. That's because the contact he made became permanent.

Map: Voyages of Discovery

For use with Worksheet 2, Unit 4

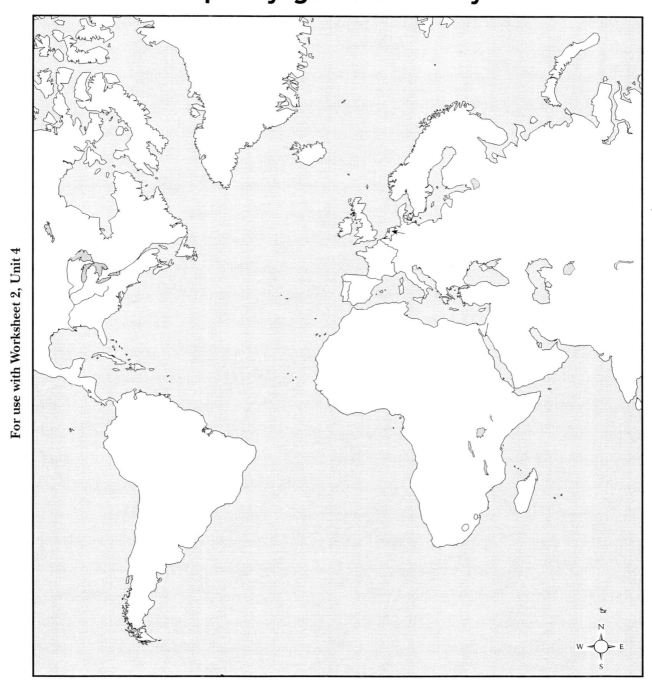

Name _____

Date _____

Voyages of Discovery

Directions: Use your Voyages of Discovery map for this activity. Trace **two** of the listed explorations from each country (but just one for the Netherlands). (Don't mark the return voyages.) Use a different color for each country's voyages. Use different-looking lines for voyages marked in the same color, to make your map easier to read. On the map, label the countries the voyages started from. Also label major continents and islands and oceans.

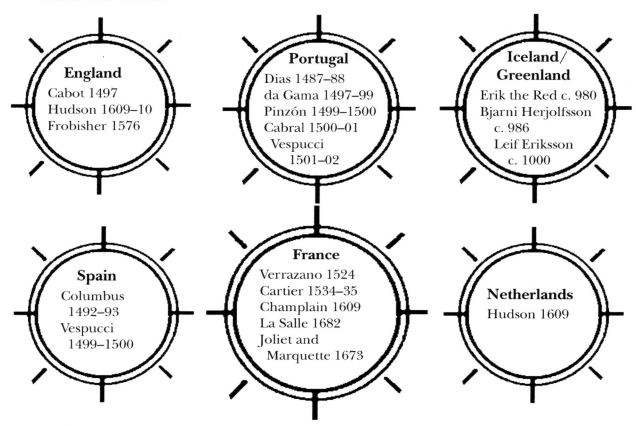

England
Cabot 1497
Hudson 1609–10
Frobisher 1576

Portugal
Dias 1487–88
da Gama 1497–99
Pinzón 1499–1500
Cabral 1500–01
Vespucci
1501–02

**Iceland/
Greenland**
Erik the Red c. 980
Bjarni Herjolfsson
c. 986
Leif Eriksson
c. 1000

Spain
Columbus
1492–93
Vespucci
1499–1500

France
Verrazano 1524
Cartier 1534–35
Champlain 1609
La Salle 1682
Joliet and
Marquette 1673

Netherlands
Hudson 1609

Extra Challenge

1. Sir Francis Drake was an Englishman who sailed for his own country, England. But sometimes an explorer sailed for a country other than his own. Identify the explorers listed above who sailed for a foreign country.

2. Exercise your math skills! Calculate the length of some of the voyages listed above, one-way and/or round-trip.

3. On a world map, show the round-the-globe voyages of Magellan and his crew and/or those of Drake.

*Focus on U.S. History:
The Era of Exploration and Discovery*

The Route East

Portugal paved the way for the Age of Exploration. Portuguese sailors learned
a lot about navigation as they fought their way over the years down Africa's west coast.

Directions: Locate and label the following landmarks on the outline map.

Madeira — 1418

Cape Bojador — 1433

Cape Blanc — 1444

Cape Verde Islands — 1444

Cape Verde — 1445

Gambia River — 1446

Ivory, Slave, Gold Coasts — 1469

Equator — 1473

Fernando Po — 1475

Congo River — 1482

Cape Cross — 1486

Cape of Good Hope — 1488

Question: Why were the Portuguese so
eager to find the southern end of Africa?

Extra Challenge:

1. Name the explorers who reached these landmarks for the first time.

2. Draw in on the map the "fearsome dangers" sailors believed would greet them
   if they sailed south of Cape Bojador.

Focus on U.S. History:
The Era of Exploration and Discovery

Boats, Boats, Boats

Overseas explorers couldn't get anywhere without seaworthy boats. Different nations facing different conditions developed different kinds of boats.

Directions: For each boat named and pictured here, tell which nation or people used it, in what waters it usually sailed, how it was well adapted to its sailors' needs, and what its disadvantages were for overseas exploring.

1. Dhow

Nation/people: _____

Where it sailed: _____

Advantages: _____

Disadvantages: _____

Nation/people: _____

Where it sailed: _____

Advantages: _____

Disadvantages: _____

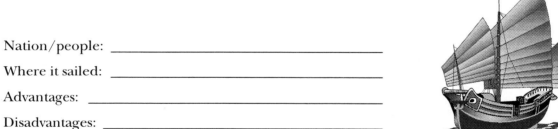

2. Junk

3. Caravel

Nation/people: _____

Where it sailed: _____

Advantages: _____

Disadvantages: _____

(continued)

Focus on U.S. History:
The Era of Exploration and Discovery

Boats, Boats, Boats *(continued)*

Nation/people: _____

Where it sailed: _____

Advantages: _____

Disadvantages: _____

4. Long ship

5. Coracle

Nation/people: _____

Where it sailed: _____

Advantages: _____

Disadvantages: _____

Nation/people: _____

Where it sailed: _____

Advantages: _____

Disadvantages: _____

6. Galley

7. Nao

Nation/people: _____

Where it sailed: _____

Advantages: _____

Disadvantages: _____

*Focus on U.S. History:
The Era of Exploration and Discovery*

Name _____

Date _____

Navigation Aids

Columbus and his fellow sailors didn't have the high-tech devices modern sailors use to find their way across the sea. Here are the simple but vital tools they used to help them navigate their way to the Americas.

Directions: Label each tool with the correct name from the list below. Then tell what each tool was used for.

compass   astrolabe   quadrant   cross staff   hourglass   knot line and float

1. Tool: _____

   Used for: _____

   _____

2. Tool: _____

   Used for: _____

   _____

3. Tool: _____

   Used for: _____

   _____

4. Tool: _____

   Used for: _____

   _____

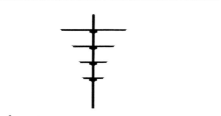

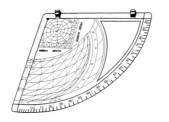

5. Tool: _____

   Used for: _____

   _____

6. Tool: _____

   Used for: _____

   _____

Extra Challenge: Explain in detail how one, some, or all of these navigational tools worked.

Name _____

Date _____

Columbus and the "Ocean Sea"

Part 1. Columbus was "admiral of the Ocean Sea"—not "Sea*s*." The following map shows you why.

Questions: What's wrong with this map? _____

How did this affect Columbus? _____

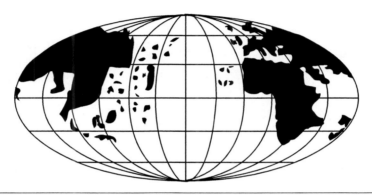

Part 2. Different parts of the Atlantic Ocean have different *prevailing*, or most frequent, **winds** and **currents**. It's very important to consider them when you're planning an ocean voyage. Columbus and the Vikings did!

Directions: Chart your own course on the map at the right, using the prevailing winds and currents (shown by the black arrows) to: (a) get from Spain to Cuba and back to Spain; and (b) get from Norway to Greenland to North America and back to Iceland or Norway.

Focus on U.S. History:
The Era of Exploration and Discovery

Name _____

Date _____

Christopher Columbus: In His Own Words

Columbus kept a detailed log (diary) of his first cross-Atlantic voyage. Here are some passages from it.*

Friday, October 12, 1492

I want the natives to develop a friendly attitude toward us because I know that they are a people who can be made free and converted to our Holy Faith more by love than by force. I therefore gave red caps to some and glass beads to others.

Saturday, October 13, 1492

I have been very attentive and have tried very hard to find out if there is any gold here. . . . I have learned that by going to the south, or rounding the island to the south, I can find a king who possesses a lot of gold and has great containers of it.

Sunday, October 14, 1492

These people are very unskilled in arms. Your Highnesses [the king and queen of Spain] will see this for yourselves when I bring to you the seven that I have taken. After they learn our language I shall return them, unless Your Highnesses order that the entire population be taken to Castile [in Spain], or held captive here. With 50 men you could subject everyone and make them do what you wished.

Tuesday, October 23, 1492

I want to leave today for the island of Cuba, which I believe to be Japan, according to the signs these people give of its magnificence

_____

* From *The Log of Christopher Columbus*, translated by Robert H. Fuson, Camden, ME: International Marine Publishing Company, 1987. Reproduced with permission of the McGraw-Hill Companies.

and wealth. . . . Since I must go where there might be great commerce, it is foolish to delay. I must move on and discover many lands, until I come across a very profitable one.

Wednesday, October 24, 1492

The Indians indicated that I should sail to the southwest to get to Cuba. And I believe them because all my globes and world maps seem to indicate that the island of Japan is in this vicinity. And I am sure that Cuba and Japan are one and the same.

Sunday, November 11, 1492

It appears to me that it would be well to take some of these people dwelling by this river to the Sovereigns, in order that they might learn our language and we might learn what there is in this country. Upon return they may speak the language of the Christians and take our customs and Faith to their people. I see and know that these people have no religion whatever, nor are they idolaters, but rather, they are very meek and know no evil. They do not kill or capture others and are without weapons . . . .

They are very trusting; they believe that there is a God in Heaven, and they firmly believe that we come from Heaven. They learn very quickly any prayer we tell them to say, and they make the sign of the cross. Therefore, Your Highnesses must resolve to make them Christians. I believe that if this effort commences, in a short time a multitude of peoples will be converted to our Holy Faith, and Spain will acquire great domains and riches and all of their villages. Beyond doubt there is a very great amount of gold in this country . . . Also, there are precious stones and pearls, and an infinite quantity of spices.

(continued)

*Focus on U.S. History:
The Era of Exploration and Discovery*

Christopher Columbus: In His Own Words *(continued)*

Tuesday, November 27, 1492

And I say that Your Highnesses must not allow any foreigner to set foot here or trade, except Catholic Christians, since it was the beginning and the end of this enterprise that it should be for the increase and the glory of the Christian religion. No one should come to these regions who is not a good Christian.

Sunday, December 16, 1492

These Indians have no arms and are naked, and have no knowledge of arms and are very timid. A thousand of them would not face three Christians, and so they are suitable to be governed and made to work and sow and do everything else that shall be necessary, to build villages and be taught to wear clothing and to observe our customs.

Tuesday, December 18, 1492

I was told that on some of these islands there is so much gold that the whole island is gold. On others they gather it and sift it with sieves and melt it to make bars, and work it in a thousand ways.

Tuesday, December 25, 1492

I certify to Your Highnesses that in all the world I do not believe there is a better people or a better country. They love their neighbors as themselves, and they have the softest and gentlest voices in the world and are always smiling.

Wednesday, December 26, 1492

I hope to God that when I come back here from Castile . . . that I will find a barrel of gold . . . and that they will have found the gold mine, and the spices, and in such quantities that within three years the Sovereigns will prepare for and undertake the conquest of the Holy Land. I have already petitioned Your Highnesses to see that all the profits of this, my enterprise, should be spent on the conquest of Jerusalem.

Sunday, January 13, 1493

The [Caribs] ran to get their bows and arrows where they had laid them and returned with cords in their hands to bind the men. The sailors were ready, since I always advised my men to be on guard; when the Indians approached, the sailors attacked. . . . In one way it troubled me and in another it did not, i.e., in that now they might be afraid of us.

What Columbus Tells Us

Directions: In his log Columbus reveals many of the reasons why Europeans became colonizers. His comments about the native Americans suggest the future pattern of European-Indian relations. Use what you've just read to answer these questions.

1. What continuing geographical mistake does Columbus make as he writes in his log?

   _____

   _____

2. What are the two main things Columbus wants to accomplish in this "New World"?

   _____

   _____

3. What "grand design" for his enterprise does Columbus reveal? _____

   _____

4. Why do you think the Indians keep telling Columbus about all the gold to be found on

   their islands? _____

   _____

5. Where did the Spanish finally find rich sources of gold? _____

   _____

6. What does Columbus think of the native Americans he meets? _____

   _____

7. What does Columbus think the relations between Spanish and native people should be like?

   _____

   _____

8. How do Columbus's words predict the future pattern of European-American Indian relations?

   _____

60   *Focus on U.S. History:*
The Era of Exploration and Discovery

Who Really Discovered America?

The ancestors of today's American Indians discovered America when they crossed the Bering land bridge tens of thousands of years ago. Who else might have discovered the Americas before Columbus arrived in 1492?

Directions: As a member of a small group, research one of the following possible early discoverers of the Americas. Gather all the information you can find that supports the claim that your subject was the earliest discoverer (after the prehistoric wanderers from Asia). Then present your case to the class.

Ancient Romans: Not known as seafarers. But Roman artifacts have turned up in Mexico and Venezuela. Were they here?

West Africans: Renowned traders, did they follow the westerly winds that would have taken them across the Atlantic?

Saint Brendan: Legend says this sixth-century Irish monk reached the "Land of Promise," where the weather never got cold. Did Brendan the Bold reach Florida or the Caribbean?

Madoc: Did this 12th-century Welsh prince really sail into the west and start a strain of "white Indians" with blue eyes?

Phoenicians: Skilled ocean traders, did they really carve messages in their ancient script on American stones?

Vikings: The Icelandic sagas tell of Norsemen in Vinland 500 years before Columbus. Is this legend or fact? Is Vinland America?

Focus on U.S. History:
The Era of Exploration and Discovery

Why Explore?

European countries sent explorers out across the hazardous seas for many reasons. These individuals chose to explore and venture to the new lands for many reasons, too.

Directions: The chart below lists a number of motives (reasons) why nations and individuals wanted to explore and colonize. Put a check mark in each box where a motive applied to a particular country. Name individual people (or groups of people) in each country who acted upon these motives.

Motive	Portugal	Spain	England
Trade routes to the East			
Religion: spread it			
Religion: practice it freely			
Acquire land			
Check rival nations' power (which ones?)			
Fame			
Fortune			
Adventure			

(continued)

Focus on U.S. History:
The Era of Exploration and Discovery

Why Explore? *(continued)*

Motive	France	Netherlands
Trade routes to the East		
Religion: spread it		
Religion: practice it freely		
Acquire land		
Check rival nations' power (which ones?)		
Fame		
Fortune		
Adventure		

Extra Challenge: Select one of the explorers whose routes you mapped in an earlier activity, or select an early colonizer. Tell what part each motive listed in the chart played in that person's exploring or colonizing.

63

Focus on U.S. History:
The Era of Exploration and Discovery

Spain and Portugal in the Americas

The objective of this unit is for students to understand the Spanish and Portuguese conquest of the Americas. Spain and Portugal led the way in exploring the "New World" that Columbus had found. Spain, in particular, rapidly established colonial settlements and plantations on the Caribbean islands. Its explorers fanned out from there to investigate Central America, South America, and large expanses of North America. The results were the fall of the mighty Aztec and Inca empires in Mexico and Peru, the subjugation of the native peoples of Central and South America, and disruption of native ways of life in North America's Southwest. The establishment of Spanish and Portuguese plantations also caused the rapid growth of African slavery in the Americas. All of these patterns were later repeated in British North America. Spanish America differed from British America, however, in an important way. The native people were not pushed out of their lands or exterminated, although many died from European diseases. In Spanish America, the races met and intermingled, creating a blended people. The activities of this unit are designed to bring students to a better understanding of the development of Hispanic America and of life in Central and South America before and after the Spanish conquest.

Student Activities

Spain Explores the Americas presents Spanish explorations in the Americas visually, by having students trace the routes of explorers on their map of the Americas. Students also identify a major accomplishment or failure of each expedition.

Mapping Mesoamerica presents the societies of Central America visually. Students locate and label peoples, places, landforms, and bodies of water on their maps and also work with a map of the great Aztec city of Tenochtitlán. A set of questions shows students how the unique siting of Tenochtitlán both helped and hindered the Aztecs when Cortés arrived.

A Noble Society asks students to chart the stratified nature of Aztec society. The Extra Challenge questions relate chart information to the ability of Spanish and Aztec societies to come together, and how that differed from the British and North American Indian experience.

Inca, Aztec, or Maya? allows students to compare and contrast pictured and labeled aspects of these three Indian civilizations.

Why Come to Spanish America? helps students understand why particular individuals might have decided to come from Spain to the Americas during the period of exploration and colonization.

Advising Cortés or Pizarro has students imagine they are advising one of the two conquistadors, explaining how they think certain factors may affect the planned conquest of the Aztec or Inca empire. Students can then compare the advice offered to the two different leaders in their different situations.

Slaves and Laborers leads students to examine the various labor systems in the Spanish Americas, by putting themselves into different individual roles and answering questions about each person's labor status and situation.

The Spanish and the Indians: Two Views presents opinions by contemporaries on how Spanish authorities treated natives of the Americas. The questions draw students into analyzing the historic debate that went on among influential people in Spain and the Americas over the Las Casas-Sepúlveda differences and arguments, with important consequences for colonialist-Indian relations. The Extra Challenge activity uses role playing to draw students further into the debate and asks them to relate it to broader issues.

Close-Up: The Black Legend examines *La Leyenda Negra* of Spanish colonialism. After background reading, students compare British and Spanish colonial policy and actions.

Spain and Portugal in the Americas

As you read in Unit 4, Spain and Portugal led the way in exploring the "New World." They also led the way in colonizing and exploiting this world and its peoples. They set a pattern that other European nations would follow, in the Americas and in Africa.

When Columbus explored the Caribbean islands, he found simple native societies. Small bands of Lucayo/Taino and Carib people lived in scattered villages among the islands. Search as he might, Columbus found no great cities filled with gold. In fact, he found little gold.

Columbus was looking in the wrong place. The central valley of Mexico and the Andes highlands of Peru, farther south, held the riches Columbus sought. They also were home to sophisticated Indian societies.

Tales of great riches lured Spanish explorers inland from their bases on Caribbean islands. **Vasco Núñez de Balboa** hacked his way across the Isthmus of Panama in **1513**. On the other side, he waded into the Pacific Ocean.

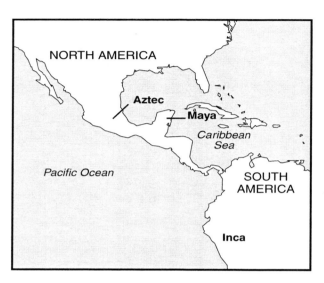

Hernán Cortés marched his army to the Aztec capital. (The size and sophistication of the city astounded Cortés and his men.) The Aztec emperor believed Cortés was the god who had vowed to return one day from over the seas to reclaim his empire. This belief, plus European weapons, horses, and disease, destroyed the great and powerful Aztec empire by **1521**.

The Maya	The Aztec	The Inca
• Lived in the Yucatán area of Mexico • Used advanced writing, math, and calendar systems • Built great ceremonial centers	• Lived in Mexico's central valley • Had a picture-writing system • Had a society run on strict class lines • Ran an empire and collected tribute from conquered peoples • Built a great city, Tenochtitlán, on an island • Were rich in gold	• Lived in the Andes highlands of Peru • Had no writing system, but built a superb network of highways for communication within the empire • Built great cities and temples • Were rich in gold and silver

(continued)

Spain and Portugal in the Americas *(continued)*

Francisco Pizarro heard about a rich empire farther south. He marched with a small army to Peru. Here, European weapons, trickery, and Incan political rivalries combined to take down the great Inca empire by **1533**.

Other Spanish explorers, including these men, trekked through large areas of today's United States.

Ponce de León—Florida

Searched for a fountain of youth, but found none.

Cabeza de Vaca—Southwest

(His name translates as "head of a cow.") Spent years in Texas as the slave of a small Indian band.

Esteban—Southwest

A black slave, very popular with most Indians, but killed by the Zuni.

Francisco Vásquez de Coronado—Southwest

Wandered from Texas to Kansas to the Grand Canyon in a search for the fabled Seven Cities of Cíbola—which didn't exist.

Hernando de Soto—Southeast

Crossed the Southeast in a fruitless, fatal search for gold.

The Spanish followed up their explorations with colonization. They had mixed motives—to spread Christianity, and to gain wealth. They set up missions in the North American Southwest. There, priests spread Christianity and made the Native Americans support the mission with their labor. In Mexico and Peru, the Spanish set up silver mines. The conquered Indians provided forced labor to work the mines. In other Spanish areas, conquistadors and Spanish colonists were given grants of land or areas of control. The Indians there had to pay tribute. They became, in effect, serfs.

Why did the Spanish come to the Americas?
"To bring light to those in darkness, and also to get rich."
—Bernal Díaz del Castillo

On the Caribbean islands, Spanish colonizers set up sugar plantations. The Indians of these islands soon died from overwork and European diseases. A new labor supply was urgently needed. Planters found their workers in Africa. The "New World" slave trade began in the 1500's and grew rapidly.

(continued)

Spain and Portugal in the Americas *(continued)*

One aspect of Spanish colonial society was very different from what would later happen in British North America. Few Spanish women came to the colonies in the early years. The conquistadors and other male colonists began to intermarry with the Indians. African slaves in Brazil and the Caribbean had opportunities to become free. They, too, intermarried. Spanish colonial society was not classless. But it did become quite mixed on many levels.

Spanish expedition arriving at the Pacific Ocean

Here are some lines from a poem by a famous poet— John Keats. He describes a key event in the Spanish exploration of the Americas:

> *Then felt I like some watcher of the skies*
>
> *When a new planet swims into his ken;*
>
> *Or like stout Cortez when with eagle eyes*
>
> *He star'd at the Pacific—and all his men*
>
> *Look'd at each other with a wild surmise—*
>
> *Silent, upon a peak in Darien.*

What's wrong with this poem?

Answer: Balboa, not Cortés, saw the Pacific from the peak in Darien.

Focus on U.S. History:
The Era of Exploration and Discovery

Map: Central, South, and North America

For use with Worksheets 2 and 3, Unit 5

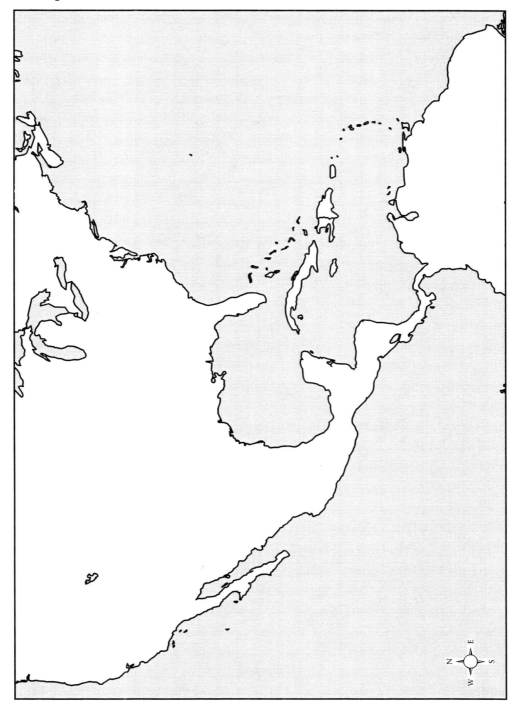

Spain Explores the Americas

Spain soon established a base on the island of Hispaniola (Haiti) in the Caribbean. From there, Spanish explorers fanned out to learn more about this "New World."

Directions: Draw the following routes of the explorations on your map of Central, South, and North America. Also, list a major accomplishment or failure of each expedition.

1. Columbus 1502
   Major accomplishment/failure: _____

2. Balboa 1510–13
   Major accomplishment/failure: _____

3. Ponce de León 1513
   Major accomplishment/failure: _____

4. Cortés 1519–21
   Major accomplishment/failure: _____

5. Narváez 1527–1528
   Major accomplishment/failure: _____

6. Pizarro 1530–33
   Major accomplishment/failure: _____

7. Cabeza de Vaca 1535–36
   Major accomplishment/failure: _____

8. de Soto 1539–42
   Major accomplishment/failure: _____

9. Coronado 1540–42
   Major accomplishment/failure: _____

10. Oñate 1596–98
    Major accomplishment/failure: _____

Mapping Mesoamerica

Part 1. Directions: **Mesoamerica** is the region of Central America where Aztec, Mayan, and other native societies flourished. On your map of Central, South, and North America, locate the peoples and places listed below.

Peoples	Cities/Towns	Landforms
Olmec	Tikal	Yucatán Peninsula
Aztec	Chichén Itzá	Cuba
Mixtec	Palenque	Sierra Madre (east and west)
Maya	Copán	
	Tula	
Present-Day Countries	Champotón	**Bodies of Water**
Mexico	Tenochtitlán	Gulf of Mexico
Honduras	Monte Albán	Pacific Ocean
Belize	Bonampak (Chiapas)	Caribbean Sea
Guatemala	Vera Cruz	Lake Texcoco
El Salvador	Tlaxcala	

(continued)

Focus on U.S. History:
The Era of Exploration and Discovery

Mapping Mesoamerica (continued)

Part 2. Directions: Here's a map of Lake Texcoco, where the Aztec capital city of Tenochtitlán was located. Locate and label the other lakes and towns around Tenochtitlán. Note the causeways that served the Aztec capital.

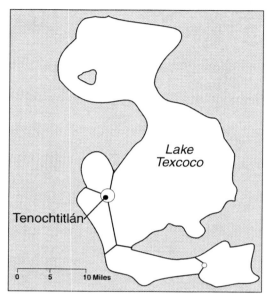

Lakes
Zumpango
Chalco
Xochimilco
Xaltocan

Towns
Texcoco
Tlacopan
Azcapotzalco
Xochimilco
Culhuacan
Chalco
Tlatelolco
Chapultepec

Questions:

1. What about Tenochtitlán's design and location made it hard for Cortés to attack and take the city?

   _____

   _____

2. What about that same design and location made the city vulnerable to Cortés's attack?

   _____

   _____

   _____

3. What role did the surrounding towns play in this conflict? _____

   _____

   _____

A Noble Society

Directions: Aztec society was structured into classes. Add the names of the classes to the chart.

Major class divisions:

Commoners
Emperor
Merchants
Slaves
Fine artisans

Other class divisions:

Nobles
Farmers
Priests
Soldiers
Fishermen
Rulers
Military leaders
Craft workers
Chiefs
Scribes
Commoners

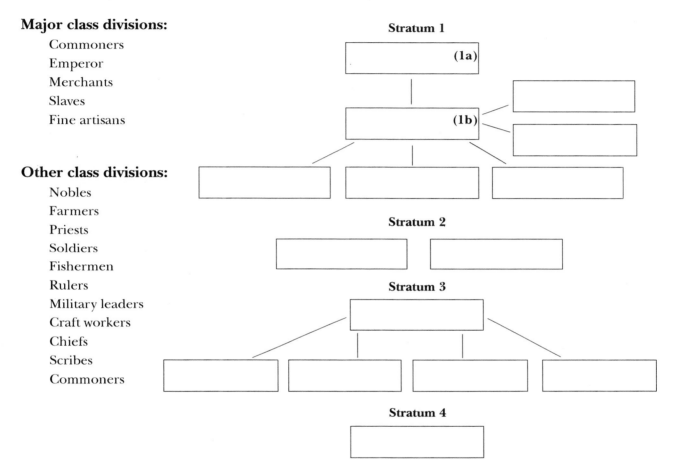

Stratum 1

(1a)

(1b)

Stratum 2

Stratum 3

Stratum 4

Extra Challenge: Answer these questions.

1. Can you see from this chart why it might have been relatively easy for the two societies, Spanish and Aztec, to begin to merge?

2. How was this merging different from the British and North American Indian experience?

Focus on U.S. History:
The Era of Exploration and Discovery

Inca, Aztec, or Maya?

Directions: Inca, Aztec, and Maya civilizations had similarities and differences. For each characteristic listed and pictured below, tell which culture (or cultures) it was part of. Write **Inca**, **Aztec**, and/or **Maya** on each line.

1. **Human sacrifice**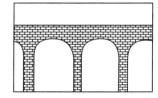

Culture: _____

2. **Ritual ball play**

Culture: _____

3. **Massive temple buildings**

Culture: _____

4. **Picture writing**

Culture: _____

5. **Very accurate calendars**

Culture: _____

6. **"Feathered serpent" god**

Culture: _____

7. **Aqueducts and canals**

Culture: _____

8. **Gold ornamental objects**

Culture: _____

9. **Large cities**

Culture: _____

10. **Empire with frequent warfare**

Culture: _____

Focus on U.S. History:
The Era of Exploration and Discovery

Why Come to Spanish America?

Directions: Many different people came to the parts of America that the Spanish were conquering and colonizing. Imagine you are each of the people described below. Explain **why you are coming to Spanish America**.

1. You are a 19-year-old black African from the Ivory Coast area, captured in intertribal warfare.

   _____

2. You are a Dominican friar (Catholic priest) from Spain; you have received some letters from your fellow friar, Bartolomé de Las Casas. _____

   _____

3. You are a conquistador who has chosen to follow Cortés. _____

   _____

4. You are the wife of a poor Spanish conquistador who left you behind in Spain.

   _____

   _____

5. You are a partner in a trading enterprise based in Madrid. _____

   _____

6. You are the younger son of a well-to-do Spanish noble family. _____

   _____

7. You are a soldier who has been fighting in the *reconquista,* the campaign to rid Spain of Islamic rule, until its recent conclusion. _____

   _____

8. You are a white Christian woman slave in Spain. _____

   _____

Advising Cortés or Pizarro

Directions: Your leader, **Hernando Cortés** or **Francisco Pizarro**, has asked your advice about conquering the **Aztec** or **Inca** empire. You realize each of the following factors could affect the outcome. What is your advice to each leader?

1. **Technology of war:** _____

_____

_____

2. **Military strategy:** _____

_____

_____

3. **Political problems within the Indian empire:** _____

_____

_____

4. **Disease:** _____

_____

_____

5. **Role of religion:** _____

_____

_____

6. **Use of trickery, treachery:** _____

_____

_____

7. **Role of terrain:** _____

_____

_____

Slaves and Laborers

The Spanish conquerors set up some special rules in their new colonies. Read about these:

encomienda: a village or area was "commended" to a Spanish colonialist, who supervised its people. He gave them military defense and religious education. In return, they owed him tribute, mostly labor and food.

requerimiento: Spanish conquerors were required to read aloud to Indians a statement. The Indians had to agree with the statement, which was that they accepted the rule of the Catholic Church and the Spanish monarchs. The Indians usually didn't understand the foreign words, so they didn't know they had to agree. Once they failed to agree, the Spanish were free to do this:
    "We shall powerfully enter into your country, and shall make war against you in all ways and manners that we can. We shall take you and your wives and your children, and shall make slaves of them. We shall take away your goods. The deaths and losses that shall result from this are your fault, and not ours."

Directions: The economies of Mesoamerica and Spanish colonial America featured various types of not-so-free labor. Imagine you are each of the following people. Answer the questions about your situation.

1. **You are an African slave on a Spanish sugar plantation in Jamaica.**

   Will your children be slaves? _____

   Are you property, owned by your master? _____

   What rights or freedoms do you have? _____

   Can you own property or buy your freedom? _____

   What caused you to become a Spanish slave? _____

   _____

2. **You are a landless Aztec peasant, before the Spanish conquest.**

   Who owns the land you work on?_____

   Are you property, a slave owned by your master? _____

   What do you owe to your master? _____

(continued)

Focus on U.S. History:
The Era of Exploration and Discovery

Slaves and Laborers *(continued)*

3. **You are a native on a Spanish colonial** *encomienda.*

    Who owns the land you work on? _____

    Are you property, a slave owned by your master? _____

    What do you owe to your master? _____

    What will happen if you can't pay what you owe to your master? _____

    _____

4. **You are an Aztec slave, before the Spanish conquest.**

    Will your children be slaves? _____

    Are you property, owned by your master? _____

    What rights or freedoms do you have? _____

    Can you own property or buy your freedom? _____

    What caused you to become a slave? _____

    _____

5. **You are the wife of an Indian warrior who has been defeated in battle
    by Cortés and his troops.**

    What is your fate? _____

6. **You are an Aztec commoner, before the Spanish conquest.**

    Who owns the land you work on? _____

    Are you a free laborer, an indentured servant, a serf, or a slave? _____

    Of what you produce on the land, do you owe anything to your ruler? _____

    _____

7. **You didn't understand a word of the** *requerimiento* **that the Spanish leader
    read to you in Spanish, or was it Latin? Later, an elder explained it to you.**

    What were you supposed to do, according to what the Spanish leader read to you?

    _____

    What terrible things could happen because you didn't understand? _____

    _____

The Spanish and the Indians: Two Views

Spanish colonial authorities often treated American Indians brutally, killing and enslaving them. Two Spanish priests spoke strongly against this. Other priests, and scholars, defended the Spanish colonial policy. This became a great debate—about slavery and about the relationship between colonial powers and the native peoples they dominated. Read what these major figures in the debate had to say.

Antón Montecino, Dominican friar (1510)

For they are God's people, these innocents, whom you destroyed. By what right do you make them die? Mining gold for you in your mines or working for you in your fields, by what right do you unleash enslaving wars upon them? They lived in peace in this land before you came, in peace in their own homes. They did nothing to harm you to cause you to slaughter them wholesale. Are you not under God's command to love them as you love yourselves? Are you out of your souls, out of your minds? Yes. And that will bring you damnation.

Bartolomé de Las Casas (1500's)

Las Casas describes the Native Americans:

God created these simple people without evil and without guile. They are the most obedient and faithful to their natural lords and to the Christians, whom they serve. They are the most submissive, patient, peaceful, and virtuous. Nor are they quarrelsome, rancorous, querulous, or vengeful. . . . They neither possess nor desire to possess worldly wealth.

Las Casas recounts Spanish treatment of the Indians:

When [the Spanish conquistadors] came into these countries, the Indians, following their custom, met them with their usual signs of joy and gladness. But the conquistadors immediately broke forth into their usual cruelties, to attain their usual aim, which was the heaping up of gold, the only god which they adore. The cities they burned to the ground. The Indian chiefs (having first tortured them), the conquistadors carried away captive, binding them in chains. Women with child, without any consideration of their weakness, the conquistadors oppressed with tedious labors and hunger, so that they died by the way. And as for the Indian children, because the women could not carry them, they were forced to throw them away, by which a number of infants were destroyed.

Focus on U.S. History:
The Era of Exploration and Discovery

The Spanish and the Indians: Two Views (continued)

Juan Ginés de Supúlveda, scholar (1500's)

Sepúlveda describes the Indians:

Now compare the Spanish gifts of prudence, talent, magnanimity, temperance, humanity, and religion with those men [the Indians] in whom you will scarcely find traces of humanity, who not only lack culture but do not even know how to write, who keep no records of their history except certain obscure and vague rememberings of some things put down in certain pictures, and who do not have written laws but only barbarous institutions and customs. And don't think that before the arrival of the Christians they were living in quiet and . . . peace. On the contrary, they were making war continuously and ferociously against each other with rage.

Sepúlveda justifies imperialism:

The man rules over the woman, the adult over the child, the father over his children . . . and so it is with the barbarous and inhumane peoples [Native Americans] who have no civil life and peaceful customs. It will always be just and in accord with natural law that such people submit to the rule of more cultured and humane princes and nations. Thanks to their virtues and the practical wisdom of their laws, the latter can destroy barbarism and educate these people to a more humane and virtuous life. And if the latter reject such rule, it can be imposed upon them by force of arms. Such a war will be just according to natural law. . . . [So] with perfect right the Spaniards rule over these barbarians of the New World . . . who in wisdom, intelligence, virtue, and humanity are as inferior to the Spaniards as infants to adults and women to men. There is as much difference between them as there is between cruel, wild peoples and the most merciful peoples . . . that is to say, between apes and men.

(continued)

Focus on U.S. History:
The Era of Exploration and Discovery

The Spanish and the Indians: Two Views *(continued)*

Directions: Answer the following questions.

1. Why is the Spanish treatment of the Native Americans wrong, according to Las Casas?

   _____

   _____

2. Why are Spanish actions justified, according to Sepúlveda? _____

   _____

   _____

3. Which groups of people in Spain and the Spanish colonies tended to side with Las Casas? Why?

   _____

   _____

4. Which groups of people in Spain and the Spanish colonies tended to side with Sepúlveda? Why?

   _____

   _____

Extra Challenge:

5. Choose an identity from among Montecino, Las Casas, Sepúlveda, their followers, and people in the middle (undecided). Debate the issue of Spanish treatment of Native Americans in the Spanish American colonies.

6. Explain how this debate applied later to the controversy over slavery, to the question of political freedom, and to later colonial experiences.

81

Focus on U.S. History:
The Era of Exploration and Discovery

Close-up: The Black Legend

England and Spain were fierce rivals in the sixteenth and seventeenth centuries. English "sea dogs" raided Spanish treasure ships. The two nations vied for control of the seas and the Americas.

During the 1650's, the Protestant Oliver Cromwell ruled England. Anti-Catholic feelings were at fever pitch, and Spain was a Catholic nation. Bartolomé de Las Casas had written a book in the 1500's about the injustices of Spanish colonialists toward the Indians. He was trying to get the Spanish government to change its policies, and he succeeded. But in 1650, nearly a hundred years after Las Casas's death, his book was published in English as *The Tears of the Indians.* Its subtitle was "An Historical and True Account of the Cruel Massacres and Slaughter of Above Twenty Millions of Innocent People, Committed by the Spaniards." The book was widely circulated as anti-Spanish propaganda.

Protestant Europe continued to spread tales of the Spanish being especially cruel and depraved as colonial rulers. Similar charges helped start the Spanish-American War in the 1890's. The Las Casas book was republished during that war. Its illustrations were grisly pictures of Spaniards torturing and murdering defenseless Indians. A Dutch artist, Theodore de Bry, created this artwork in the sixteenth century. He had never visited the Americas. Anti-Spanish feelings also played a large part in the Texas revolt of 1836 and the Mexican-American War of 1846–48.

This distorted anti-Hispanic stereotype is called *La Leyenda Negra,* the Black Legend, of Spanish colonialism. It has fed anti-Hispanic sentiments over the years. In fact, Spanish colonialists didn't slaughter native Americans wholesale. They did kill a lot by warfare and abuse, but they killed many more by disease, unwittingly, just as British and other European colonists did. The abuses Las Casas complained about were bad, and they did happen, but they were corrected. And the record of British and Native American relations could be considered a Black Legend of its own.

Directions: Compare British and Spanish treatment of and relations with the natives of the Americas—in a written report, in chart form, or in a class discussion/debate.

Some Conclusions

The objectives of this unit are to guide students to an overall understanding of the theme of this book: how three worlds meet and mingle as Europe, Africa, and the Americas come together at last. This unit draws on knowledge gained from previous units and activities in this book; it should help students draw broader conclusions and make connections with the information they have gathered and absorbed so far.

Student Activities

The Columbian Exchange helps students identify the many interchanges among Europe, Africa, and America that resulted from the meeting initiated by Columbus.

What They Discovered helps students realize the amazing variety of previously unknown and impressive things that the Europeans found when they finally reached the Americas. For reinforcement, make sure that students have previously located these things on their maps.

The Human Cost uses line graphs to show the dramatic drops in native populations in three areas of the Americas after European contact. The following worksheet (Reading the Human Cost Graphs) guides students in reading and interpreting the graphs to learn more about the tragic cost of this interworld contact.

The Age of Exploration Changes Europe is an individual or small-group activity that leads to an understanding of how the Age of Exploration did not just affect American peoples, but also caused profound changes in Europe.

Combined Time Line gives a frame for connecting the many events explored in this book as they affected the four main areas of the world—Europe, America, Asia, and Africa.

Who Am I? uses a game format to test students' recognition of 24 early explorers.

Some Conclusions

Contact among Europeans, Americans, and Africans changed every society it touched. In some cases, results were tragic. Native Americans had no immunity to European diseases. (Africans did. Europeans and Africans had not been totally separated for tens of thousands of years.) Indians in the Americas were killed in astounding numbers by diseases such as measles, chickenpox, smallpox, and influenza (flu).

Also, Europeans thought they had a right to take over lands occupied by

- Non-Christians
- People who didn't "improve" the land
- "Uncivilized" people

So, the Europeans imposed their own ideas on the native populations. They tried to wipe out native cultures. Sometimes they did this with good intentions, convinced that they were saving natives' souls by bringing Christianity to them.

Europeans also brought Africans to the Americas as slaves. They ignored the Africans' native culture, forcing the African slaves into a new culture. The slave trade caused a massive population shift. As many as 10 to 12 million Africans left their native continent for the Americas during the slave trading era.

Europeans, Africans, and Americans, now that they were living together, began to change one another. The mingling of these three peoples changed each one. The world's population moved all around. For the first time, empires spanned the ocean. Global trade began. Slavery boomed on a scale unknown before in history. Population and living patterns in Europe changed. Our American society was born.

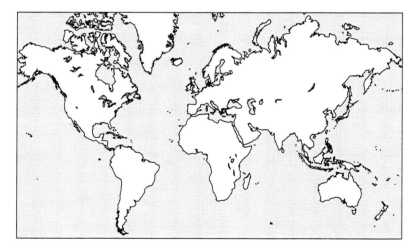

84

Focus on U.S. History:
The Era of Exploration and Discovery

Name _____

Date _____

The Columbian Exchange

The exchange of cultural and natural items among Europeans, Native Americans, and the Africans who soon joined them is called the **Columbian Exchange**. That's because the arrival of Columbus in the "New World" started a **three-way meeting of cultures**.

Directions: Draw a line from each item to show the continent(s) it originally came from. Draw another line to show the continent(s) it went to.

Animals
  horses
  cows
  pigs
  turkeys
  sheep
  goats
  parrots
  chickens

Human-made Items
  guns, gunpowder
  metal tools (machetes, plows)
  hammocks
  wheel (carts, wagons)
  precious-metal crafts

Food products
  sugarcane, cane sugar
  potatoes
  onions, radishes, lettuce
  bananas
  coffee
  tobacco
  wheat, barley, rye, oats
  maize
  melons

Ideas
  about geography
  about democracy

The Americas

Europe

Africa

85

Focus on U.S. History:
The Era of Exploration and Discovery

What They Discovered

Directions: The European explorers discovered many wonderful things that they had never known before. (Of course, the peoples living in the Americas knew that these things were here—at least the things near where they lived!) Here's an Extra Challenge activity. Alone or in a small group, identify as many examples as possible of the following items that the Europeans found in their "New World" and had not ever seen before.

Major Landforms:	Major Water Bodies:
Plants:	**Animals:**
Peoples:	**Natural Resources:**

Follow-up: Be sure that all of these items are on the various maps that you completed in previous units.

Focus on U.S. History:
The Era of Exploration and Discovery

The Human Cost

Directions: Warfare. Forced labor and slavery. Destruction of the native environment. All had harsh effects on the native population of the Americas. But by far the biggest, deadliest killer was disease. Native Americans had no immunities to many European diseases. The Europeans had no idea they were bringing microbes to the New World that would kill off most of the peoples they met there. Study these graphs.

1. NATIVE POPULATION OF NEW ENGLAND DURING EARLY YEARS OF COLONIZATION

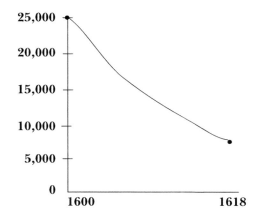

2. ARAWAK POPULATION OF HISPANIOLA DURING FIRST 50 YEARS OF COLONIZATION

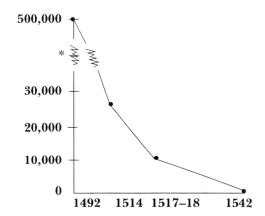

3. NATIVE POPULATION OF MEXICO DURING FIRST CENTURY OF SPANISH OCCUPATION

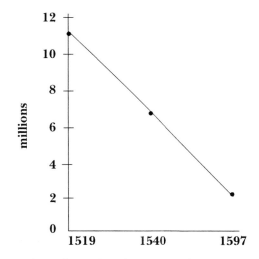

* Marks indicate break in span of years.

Focus on U.S. History:
The Era of Exploration and Discovery

Reading the Human Cost Graphs

Directions: Using the Human Cost graphs, answer the
following questions about the drop in native American
populations after European contact.

1. How many native Americans lived in Hispaniola when Columbus arrived?

   _____ How many in 1514? _____

   How many in 1542? _____

2. The native population in Mexico fell from _____ to

   _____ from 1519 to 1597. How many fewer Mexican natives were

   alive in 1597 than in 1519? _____ than in 1540? _____

3. By about how much did the New England native population drop from 1600 to 1618?

   by one half? by one third? by four fifths? by nine tenths? by two thirds?

   (Circle the correct answer.)

4. Which population group suffered the greatest numerical loss? _____

5. What important event occurred in Hispaniola in 1492? _____

   _____

6. What important event occurred in Mexico in 1519? _____

   _____

7. Did the arrival of the Pilgrims in Massachusetts account for most of the deaths

   shown on the New England graph? _____

   If not, what did? _____

Focus on U.S. History:
The Era of Exploration and Discovery

Name _____

Date _____

The Age of Exploration Changes Europe

Contact with Europeans greatly changed African and native American societies. But the Age of Exploration, and contact with these new peoples and lands, greatly changed Europe, too.

Directions: Individually, or in a small group, select one or more of the topics listed below. Do some research. Then explain how the era of exploration caused changes in Europe in that (or those) area(s).

Knowledge of geography	**What people ate and drank**
Religious thought	**Patterns of European political power**
Ideas about government	**Medieval thought patterns**
European economy	**European nationalism**
Approaches to science	

Focus on U.S. History:
The Era of Exploration and Discovery

Combined Time Line

Directions: Sometimes it's hard to make connections among events happening in different parts of the world. Here's a good way to make those connections for the events you've been learning about in this book. Make a combined time line, in the form of a chart. You might be surprised to see what's happening at the same times in opposite sections of the globe. This is your pattern:

Years	Americas	Africa	Europe	Asia

Focus on U.S. History:
The Era of Exploration and Discovery

Who Am I?

Directions: Form teams, cut out these cards, and play a "Who Am I?" game. Teams take turns drawing cards and reading them aloud. Can the other team answer "Who Am I?" correctly?

Francisco Vásquez de Coronado (1540–42)
 	
   I led an expedition into the Southwest of North America. We searched in vain for the Seven Cities of Gold for two long years. We returned to Mexico City empty-handed. Who am I?
	Leif Ericsson (c. 1000)
	
	   I sailed from Greenland to Vinland 500 years before Columbus crossed the Atlantic, but I didn't stay very long. Who am I?

Vasco da Gama (1497–99)
 	
   I made the first round trip by sea between Portugal and the Spice Islands. It was tough getting around the Cape of Good Hope! Who am I?
	Bartholomeu Dias (1487–88)
	
	   They said it couldn't be done, but I did it! I found the southern end of Africa and sailed a little way beyond it. The route to the Indies is now open. Who am I?

Henry Hudson (1609–10)
 	
   I made great discoveries in North America for the Dutch and for the English. I even got a river and a bay named for me. But my ship's crew set me adrift in a small boat, and I disappeared. Who am I?
	John Cabot (1497)
	
	   I'm an Italian sailor known by an English name. I was the first European after the Vikings to find North America, but most people forget to give me credit for this. Who am I?

Ferdinand Magellan (1519–22)
 	
   I had a grand idea: to sail all the way around the world! Unfortunately, I got in the middle of a fight between native groups in the Philippines and was killed. But one of my boats did finish the voyage. Who am I?
	Christopher Columbus (1492–93)
	
	   I figured out the best way to get to the Indies: by sailing west across the "Ocean Sea." And I succeeded! I didn't find the Great Khan, but I did find lots of Indians and islands. Who am I?

(continued)

Who Am I? *(continued)*

Amerigo Vespucci (1499–1502) I sailed across the "Ocean Sea" twice, while Columbus was making his later voyages. Little did I know when I wrote about my trips that my name would be given to this "New World." Who am I?	**Giovanni da Verrazano (1524)** I'm an Italian who sailed to the Americas for the king of France. While I sailed along the North American coast, I discovered the entrance to the harbor of what you now call New York. Thanks for naming the world's longest suspension bridge for me! Who am I?
La Salle (1682) My real name is René-Robert Cavelier, and I paddled down the Mississippi River to the Gulf of Mexico in a canoe. This gave my country, France, claim to all the lands west of the Mississippi—a huge territory. Who am I?	**Pedro Alvares Cabral (1500–01)** I set out to follow the sea route around Africa. But I sailed a little too far west, and discovered Brazil instead. This gave my country of Portugal a vast and rich American colony. Who am I?
Vitus Bering (1741) I'm a Danish sailor who found and claimed Alaska for Russia. In return, I got a strait and a sea named for me. Who am I?	**Jacques Cartier (1534–35)** I'm a Frenchman who sailed up the great Saint Lawrence River, opening Canada for exploration and settlement by Europeans. Who am I?
Louis Joliet and Père (Father) Jacques Marquette (1673) We paddled our way through the Great Lakes and found the Mississippi River. Now our nation, France, had a water route from the Atlantic Ocean all the way through the heart of the North American continent. Who are we?	**Samuel de Champlain (1609)** I'm a Frenchman who paddled by canoe into a large lake that's now named after me. I was the first European in the land you now call New York. Who am I?

(continued)

Focus on U.S. History:
The Era of Exploration and Discovery

Who Am I? *(continued)*

Martin Frobisher (1576–78) I made three fruitless voyages to northern North America in the 1500's. My sponsors, the English queen and merchants, hoped I'd find the fabled Northwest Passage to the Spice Islands. Who am I?	**Francis Drake (1579–81)** I grabbed gold and silver from Spanish ships and settlements on the west coast of South and Central America in the 1500's. Then I sailed up the coast and explored North America's west coast, making claims here for England. Who am I?
Vasco Núñez de Balboa (1513) I stowed away with my dog on an expedition to colonize the Panama area. I became a leader, crossed the Isthmus of Panama, and found the Pacific Ocean. Who am I?	**Hernando Cortés (1519–21)** I led an expedition to Mexico to discover great treasures, and I found them. I defeated the great Aztec empire without much opposition. Who am I?
Francisco Pizarro (1532–33) I was old for my time—nearly sixty!—but I marched my men to Peru. I tricked the Inca ruler, took him captive, and conquered the mighty Inca empire. Who am I?	**Juan Ponce de León (1513)** I was so impressed with all the flowers in the land I explored, I named this region La Florida. But the natives fought my expedition everywhere I went, and they finally killed me. Who am I?
Alvar Núñez Cabeza de Vaca (1528–36) I barely survived an expedition to Florida. I was a slave of poor Indians in Texas for years. Then I escaped and explored a lot of the Southwest. Who am I?	**Hernando de Soto (1539–42)** I led my men on a horribly difficult trek through the Southeast. I thought we'd failed, and I died. But I'd found the Mississippi River! Who am I?

Focus on U.S. History:
The Era of Exploration and Discovery

Answers,
Additional Activities,
and Assessments

Unit 1: The Americas and Early Americans

Early Migrations and Peoples

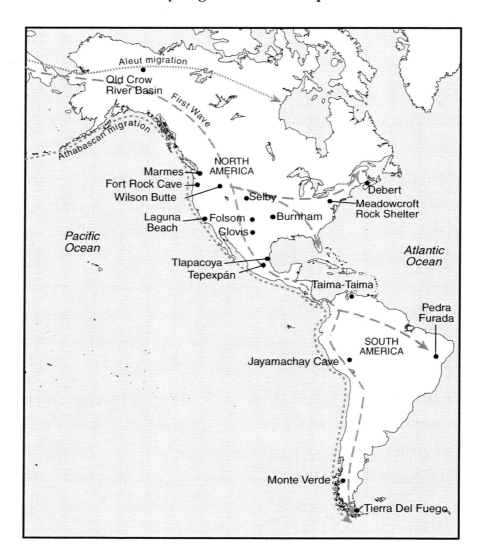

Filling Out the Map

A Variety of Dwellings

Longhouse
People: Iroquois
Region: New York State area
Materials: Bark shingles over wooden poles
Reason: Available materials, multifamily, expresses tribal unity

Adobe buildings
People: Pueblo
Region: Southwest
Materials: Stone/adobe or adobe/pole
Reason: Available materials, well suited to desert climate, promoted group living, provided good security against raiders

Domed snow house
People: Eskimo/Inuit
Region: Arctic
Materials: Snow blocks

Reason: Available material, excellent insulation against the cold

Chickee
People: Seminole
Region: Southeast
Materials: Poles, palm leaves
Reason: Raised away from wet ground, insects, snakes; sides can be pulled up in hot weather; available materials

Tepee
People: Plains Indians
Region: Great Plains
Materials: Poles, animal skins
Reason: Easily put up and taken down by nomadic people; available materials

Earth lodge
People: Pawnee and others
Region: Missouri River region, mid-Plains
Materials: Posts, brush, thatch, and earth

Reason: Provided home for extended
families; available materials

Rectangular wooden plank house
People: Northwest Coast groups
(Kwakiutl, etc.)
Region: Northwest Coast
Materials: Wooden logs and planks
Reason: Abundant available materials;
well suited to mild climate where people
had time to build substantial structures;
provided group living quarters

Domed wigwam
People: Many, including Algonquian-
speaking groups
Region: Far West, Middle West prairies,
other areas
Materials: Poles covered with woven or sewn
mats, bark, sometimes hides, thatch
Reason: Coverings could be taken along
when moving camp; available materials;
flexible as to style and materials used

A Typical Village

G   Cornfield

C   Dance

K   Cooking fire

I   Vegetable garden

L   Fishing spot

H   Sprouting field

A   Hut

F   Live scarecrow

J   Hunt

B   Ceremonial fire

E   Tobacco fields

D   Feast

The All-Purpose Animal

Brain: hide and skin softener

Horns: cups, spoons, bowls, dishes, toy tops,
decoration, storage pouches

Hide/skin: clothing, tepee covers, bags and
other containers, drums, boat covers,

shields, blankets, bedding, cradle boards,
snowshoes, riding equipment (lariat,
bridle, etc.)

Hair: weaving, rope, stuffing, ornaments

Bones: spoons, small tools (e.g., scrapers, awls),
whistles, digging tools, dice, handles,
weapons, knives, pipes, sleds
—marrow as part of pemmican

Liver: eaten raw after hunt

Intestine: pemmican sausage casing,
bowstrings, cord

Tail: flyswatter

Dung: campfire fuel

Tendons: thread, cord

Bladder: jugs for carrying liquids, pemmican
sausage casing, storage pouches

Stomach: container for cooking or carrying
liquids

Hooves: glue (after boiling), implements,
jewelry, utensils

Sinew: bowstrings, rope, thread

Tongue: food

Blood: edible liquid

Teeth: small tools

Meat: food—cooked or dried as jerky, or
pounded fine and mixed with bone marrow,
fat, and berries to become pemmican

Speaking in Signs

Have students compare this type of signing
with today's American Sign Language.

People and Places

When charts are completed, show students
how they fit together into one large chart:

Chart 1	Chart 2
Chart 3	Chart 4

This would make a good group activity.
Make different groups responsible for charting

particular areas, then bring them together to make a final, complete chart.

You could also have students, individually or in groups, chart the differences between Native Americans of two very different areas, such as the Southwest and the Great Forest, or the Subarctic and the Southeast. This would illustrate the great variation in habitats on the continent that caused great differences in cultures, without having to work through an entire four-page chart.

Chart 1

Area	Geography/ Climate	Type of Sustenance	Shelter
Arctic	tundra, extreme cold	hunting	domed snow houses; snow-earth houses; underground sod houses
Subarctic	mountains, tundra, taiga, severe climate	game (nomadic hunting)	tepees
Northwest Coast	coast and forest, moderate to chilly, dense rainfall	little agriculture, much fishing and hunting	elaborate, decorated wooden houses
Plateau	mostly high, flat land; harsh, cold climate with deserts and canyons	hunting, gathering, fishing, trade	underground pit-house villages
Great Basin	arid basin, snowy ranges	scarce seasonal resources: subsistence (foraging, small game, fish)	nomadic shelters

Chart 2

Area	Social Structure/ Government	Major Tribal Groups/Peoples	Typical Handicrafts
Arctic	small family groups	Aleuts, Inuits	ivory carvings, masks
Subarctic	small family groups and bands	Algonquian speakers (Cree, Ojibwa), Athabascan	
Northwest Coast	matrilineal; elaborate social structure (chiefs, nobles, etc.)	Kwakiutl, Haida, Tlingit	wood carvings, totem poles, elaborate ritual objects
Plateau	family groups	Shoshone, Nez Percé	baskets
Great Basin	family groups	Paiute, Ute, Shoshone, Bannock	baskets

Chart 3

Area	Geography/ Climate	Type of Sustenance	Shelter
California	fertile soil, moderate temperatures	small game, nuts, fish (hunter-gatherers)	dome or cone houses
Southwest	rugged mesas, mountains, arid, hot semidesert; cold nights	dryland agriculture; (hunter-raiders: Apache and Navajo)	adobe/stone apartment houses
Great Plains	grasslands	buffalo hunting, some farming	tepees, earth lodges
Great Forest	thick forest, rivers, lakes; cold, snowy winters	fishing, hunting, farming	wood/bark houses, some longhouses
Southeast	mild, humid subtropics	farming, hunting, fishing	palisaded villages

Chart 4

Area	Social Structure/ Government	Major Tribal Groups/Peoples	Typical Handicrafts
California	isolated tribes, small bands	hundreds	basket weaving
Southwest	matrilineal clans	Hopi, Zuni, Navajo, Pueblo, Apache	pottery, turquoise and shell jewelry, cotton and wool weaving
Great Plains	clan/tribe, elected leaders	Arapaho, Sioux, Cheyenne, Blackfoot	bead and quill work
Great Forest	clans, council of elders; power passes matrilineally	Powhatan, Delaware, Iroquois, Miami, Huron, Algonquin, Ottawa, Shawnee	bead and quill work
Southeast	chiefs chosen for wisdom and guidance	Seminole, Creek, Cherokee, Chickasaw, Choctaw, Yamasee	cane items, baskets

Digging Up the Past

Layer 1: U.S. silver dollar

Layer 2: Spanish gold coin, horse ribs

Layer 3: seed corn

Layer 4: Plains bison skull, pottery shards

Layer 5: mammoth tusk, giant bison horn, Clovis spear point

Layer 6: dinosaur backbone

Native American Culture

1. <u>Religious beliefs and practices:</u> spiritual life is part of everyday life; spiritual forces present in nature, all things; bad spiritual forces must be placated

2. <u>Community:</u> government by elders, by consensus; great loyalty to the tribe

3. <u>Food sources and types:</u> agriculture (corn), hunting, fishing, plus gathering of wild foods like groundnuts and acorns

4. <u>Role of trade and handicrafts:</u> conduct trade with far-away groups; value strength and beauty in the items they make for everyday use, like wampum belts, trays, kettles, spoons, canoes.

5. <u>Gender roles:</u> men hunt, fish, conduct war; women do the agricultural work

6. <u>Social and physical characteristics:</u> gentle, friendly, hospitable, enjoy entertainments, wise, independent; physically are black-haired, tall, well-built, with skin darker than that of Europeans

Additional Activity Suggestions

You could have students do any of the following additional activities.

1. *You, the teacher:* Display pictures or illustrations of Native American artifacts— artistically shaped and decorated objects used for everyday tasks or special ceremonies. Choose objects that represent different peoples. Individually or in groups, have students identify each object, tell which Native peoples made and used it, what it is made of, and why it was used.

2. *Students:* Find and retell Native American creation stories. *Teacher:* Ask how each might have been inspired by actual events, how each represents the group's origins in allegory, how each expresses the group's values and beliefs.

3. *Students:* Gather evidence about the earliest recorded Native American group that lived in your area. Make this into a display to be shown in school.

4. *Students:* With classmates, demonstrate some games that Indian young people enjoyed playing.

5. *Teacher:* Read all or parts of Henry Wadsworth Longfellow's *The Song of Hiawatha.* *Students:* Does this paint an accurate portrait of the Indian people Longfellow was writing about?

6. *Students:* Create a time line of significant events from the peopling of the North and South American continents to 1500. (Teacher Note: Unit 6 has students create a combined time line. You could lead up to that activity by having students create time lines for Units 1 through 5.)

Assessment

1. Were Native American societies "primitive," as early European visitors often described them, or complex? Answer this question with many specific details about aspects of Native American culture, such as political and social structure, economic systems, and spiritual beliefs.

2. Select one category from the Peoples and Places chart, such as shelter or handicrafts. Write an essay describing in detail the differences and similarities among Native American cultures on the topic you chose.

Unit 2: African Roots

Mapping Peoples and Places

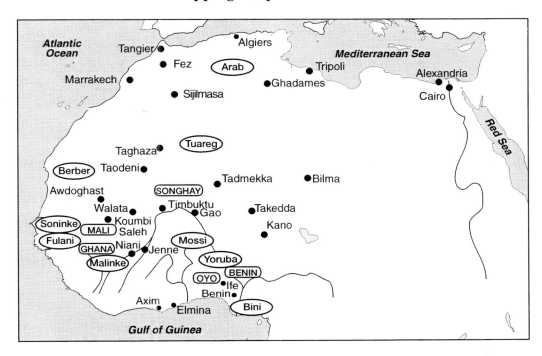

Mapping African Trade

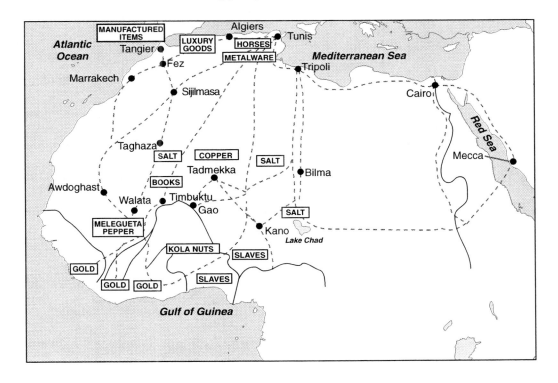

The West African Land

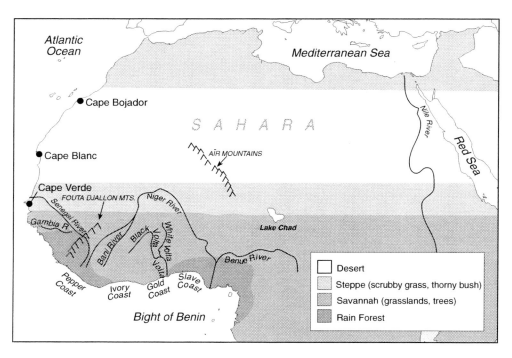

Two Kinds of Religions

Prayer/Religious Buildings

Islam: Pray five times a day at specified times; preferably, males gather at a mosque, a substantial building

African: Pray as called for; no monumental religious buildings, only simple shrines

Food/Eating

Islam: Fast during the month of Ramadan; observe Koranic dietary restrictions (no pork; no blood; no food from an animal that dies of itself, is beaten to death, is strangled, is killed by a fall, is gored by a horn, or has been eaten by other animals; rules suspended if needed to save a life)

African: No particular religious dietary restrictions

God(s)

Islam: One supreme God only, Allah

African: Generally, one supreme God, with many lesser gods and spirits who actually run the physical world and affect people's lives

Women's Roles

Islam: Women must be veiled in public, must have no contact with men outside their family

African: Women generally have full participation in village and city life, even trading at the marketplace; go about naked if slaves, virgins, or prepubescents

Slavery

Islam: No slavery for free Muslims (but slaves who convert remain slaves)

African: Slaves could usually buy their freedom, serve in the military, marry, accumulate goods, become leaders

Toleration of Other Religions:

Islam: Prescribes *jihads* (holy wars) against unbelievers (infidels)

African: Tolerant of all religious beliefs

Men's Work, Women's Work

Students can use the information they generate in this activity to help complete the Unit 3 chart, Three Worlds About to Meet.

(Note: Gender role answers given here are generalizations. Individual societies varied somewhat.)

Food production

Planting and tending crops: men and women
Harvesting crops: women
Processing foods: women
Hunting for meat: men
Fishing: men

Making things

Making pots: women and men
Making baskets: women and men
Weaving: women and men
Making tools: men
Making weapons: men
Making utensils: women and men

Village tasks

Clearing land: men
Building houses: men
Tending chickens: women

Commerce

Marketing surplus crops: men and women
Trading other goods: men and women
Mining gold: men and women
Serving in the military: men

The African-American Food Swap

Maize: America to Africa
Yams: Africa to America
Peanuts: America to Africa
Tomatoes: America to Africa
Millet: Africa to America
Melegueta pepper: Africa to America
Cacao: America to Africa
Sorghum: Africa to America
Rice: Africa (originally from Asia) to America
Squash varieties: America to Africa
Okra: Africa to America
Bean varieties: America to Africa

Cities of the African Empires

Answers will vary depending on the European city selected for comparison.

African Buildings

1. Materials: mud and thatch
   Reason: available materials; mud insulates from heat; storage bin up on stones to protect food inside from animals

2. Materials: adobe (sun-dried mud and straw, or clay)
   Reason: available materials; flat-roofed from Arab/Islamic design; interior protected from extreme heat; protruding wooden posts serve as permanent scaffolding for repairs

3. Materials: mud and thatch; wooden stilts
   Reason: available materials; on stilts for protection from vermin, snakes, and flooding

4. Extra Challenge: This is from a contemporary view of Timbuktu, showing the combination of traditional domed African mud-and-thatch dwellings and the flat-roofed adobe Arab/Islamic style. The latter came into vogue when es-Saheli came back to Timbuktu with Mansa Musa.

Additional Activity Suggestions

You could have students do any of the following additional activities.

1. Read and retell some West African folk tales (you might do the retelling to a group of younger students). What do these tales tell about traditional West African life, in areas such as family organization, gender roles, political/social systems, food, work, play, and so on?

2. Find and read more descriptions of the great African empires and cities written by people who visited them, like the selections on worksheet 8. You could use what you read to create illustrations and/or models of the cities and their inhabitants.

3. Create a class display of West African art and handicrafts, labeling your display items to explain which people made each object, what materials were used, and how it expresses characteristics of that people's society and culture.

4. Make a chart comparing slavery in Africa and in the Americas.

5. Create a time line of significant events in West and central African history to 1500. (*Teacher Note:* Unit 6 has students create a combined time line. You could lead up to that activity by having students create time lines for Units 1 through 5.)

Assessment

Many Europeans called Africa the "dark continent" and considered the Africans they took into slavery as "primitive" and "pagan." Explain in detail why this view of Africans and African culture was inaccurate.

Unit 3: Western Europe on the Eve of Exploration

East-West Trade

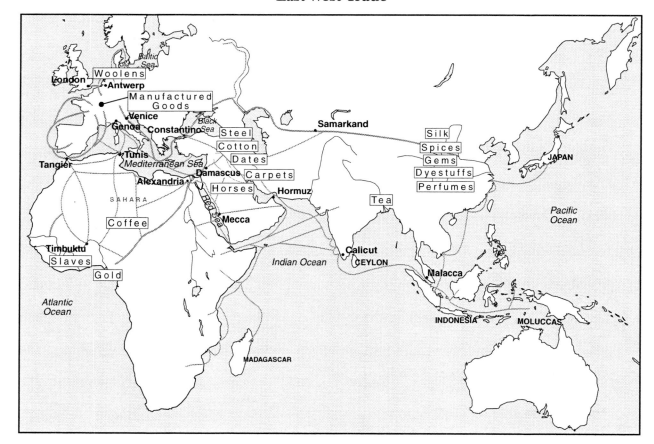

Spurs to the Age of Exploration

You could assign just one or two events/developments per small group. Groups could then report orally.

Renaissance: Inspired individual accomplishment; fired people's imaginations; emphasized fact-based approach to knowledge (explore! find out what's out there); classical texts about world geography were rediscovered.

Protestant Reformation: Caused religious wars, rivalry to secure colonial lands for Catholic or Protestant governments; inspired followers to become colonial settlers, either to spread their own religious faith or to practice it without persecution.

Strong central governments: Consolidated power, created internal stability. Countries became wealthy and could now look beyond their own borders.

Black Death: Hastened end of feudalism; serfs left the land, moved to cities, started to build the urban economy that fueled exploration.

Spread of Islam: With the fall of Constantinople, the overland route to the East was closed to Europeans. New routes—around Africa, west across the Atlantic—had to be found.

Crusades: Created a European demand for many eastern goods; spurred trade; whetted Europeans' taste for conquest and adventure; inspired religious zeal; made Italian city-states, which provided financial backing for exploration expeditions, wealthy and powerful.

Reconquista of Spain: Christianizing the "pagans" of the Americas was a natural extension of this Christian offensive against infidels.

Printing: New, old, and popular knowledge and theory become widely available.

The Countries of Europe

England
   Main religion: Protestant/Catholic (changed according to ruler)
   Main language: English
   Type of government: Monarchy, with Parliament gaining power

France
   Main religion: Catholic
   Main language: French
   Type of government: Absolute monarchy

Spain
   Main religion: Catholic
   Main language: Spanish
   Type of government: Absolute monarchy

Portugal
   Main religion: Catholic
   Main language: Portuguese
   Type of government: Absolute monarchy

Italy
   Main religion: Catholic
   Main language: Italian
   Type of government: Mostly individual city-states

Netherlands
   Main religion: Multi-sect Protestant (Dutch Reformed)
   Main language: Dutch
   Type of government: Nonresident monarchy (Spain and Holy Roman Empire), but strong local government

Three Worlds About to Meet

This is a good small-group activity. Students can jot notes on their charts as they discuss general characteristics for each category. Then they can develop another chart, or other visual, to display their conclusions.

Additional Activity Suggestions

You could have students do any of the following additional activities.

1. Working in a small group, research and report on one of the following aspects of European life in the 1400's and 1500's: family organization, gender roles, ways of earning a living, relationship to the

environment, education, or ideas about other cultures.

2. Create a class display of Renaissance artwork that expresses both the spirit of individualism and inquiry and the rise of the merchant classes in Europe that fueled the Age of Exploration.

3. Create a time line of significant events in Europe from 1300 to 1500. (Teacher Note: Unit 6 has students create a combined time line. You could lead up to that activity by having students create time lines for Units 1 through 5.)

Assessment

1. From what you have read and what you see on your trade routes map, explain why Eastern goods were so expensive to buy in Europe.

2. Write an essay explaining the many different aspects of Western European society that promoted overseas exploration.

Unit 4: The Early Explorers

Voyages of Discovery

(Students will show two of the listed explorations for each country, and one for the Netherlands, on their map.)

Sailing from England

Cabot 1497—to Canada (Newfoundland)

Hudson 1609–10—to Hudson's Bay, Canada

Frobisher 1576—to Baffin Island, Canada

Sailing from Spain

Columbus 1492–93—to the Caribbean islands

Vespucci 1499–1500—to northern coast of South America, Caribbean

Sailing from Portugal

Dias 1487–88—to Cape of Good Hope, Africa

Da Gama 1497–99—around Cape of Good Hope to India

Pinzón 1499–1500—mouth of Amazon River, Brazil

Cabral 1500–1501—to Brazil's east coast, then on to India

Vespucci 1501–1502—east coast of South America from Brazil south

Sailing from France

Verrazano 1524—to east coast of North America, up along coast to Newfoundland

Cartier 1534–35—to Newfoundland and St. Lawrence River

Champlain 1609—into St. Lawrence River

La Salle 1682—down the Mississippi to the Gulf of Mexico (started from eastern end of Lake Ontario, not from France)

Jolliet and Marquette 1673—across Lake Michigan, down Wisconsin River, then down Mississippi River to below the Arkansas River (did not start this expedition from France)

Sailing from Iceland/Greenland

Erik the Red c. 980—Iceland to Greenland

Bjarni Herjolfsson c. 986—from Greenland to Vinland (Newfoundland, probably; possibly Nova Scotia, Labrador, and/or New England)

Leif Eriksson c. 1000—from Greenland to Vinland

Sailing from the Netherlands

Hudson 1609—to Barents Sea, then to south of Nova Scotia, along coast to Hudson River, up river

The Route East

Extra Challenge: Some explorers' names:

Cape Bojador—Gil Eannes
Cape Blanc—Nuno Tristão
Cape Verde Islands—Dinís Dias
Cape Verde—Tristão
Gambia River—Tristão
Ivory, Slave, Gold Coasts—Fernão Gomes
Equator—Gonçalves
Congo River—Diogo Cão
Cape Cross—Diogo Cão
Cape of Good Hope—Bartholomeu Dias

    Extra Challenge: Among the terrors were, near the equator, boiling-hot seas and a sun that would burn you black. Beyond this was a region where only fearsome monsters lived.

Boats, Boats, Boats

1. <u>Dhow</u>
   Nation/people: Arabs
   Where: Indian Ocean
   Advantages: Used lateen sail, so could sail close to the wind; could be restitched to repair
   Disadvantages: Hard to keep on course, steered by oar; held together with fiber and wooden pegs, so weaker on open sea

2. <u>Junk</u>
   Nation/people: China
   Where: Mostly Asian waters and Indian Ocean
   Advantages: Large, could carry a lot of cargo; very seaworthy; comfortable; efficient sails; watertight holds

Disadvantages: Had to sail with the wind behind it

3. Caravel
    Nation/people: Southern Europeans, especially Portugal and Spain
    Where: Atlantic, Mediterranean
    Advantages: Lateen rigging, so could sail close to the wind; sturdy; small, very maneuverable, with rudder for steering
    Disadvantages: Small, with limited space for cargo, supplies, crew

4. Long ship
    Nation/people: Vikings
    Where: Scandinavian waters, to Iceland
    Advantages: Fast; seaworthy; fine for long sea voyages
    Disadvantages: Small cargo capacity; square sail; oar steering

5. Coracle
    Nation/people: Ireland
    Advantages: Light, sturdy for coastal waters
    Disadvantages: Primitive steering; very hard to navigate; some powered only by oars; low, not good for long ocean voyages

6. Galley
    Nation/people: Mediterranean Sea area
    Advantages: Long and narrow, suitable for Mediterranean waters; generally used oars rather than sails, so could operate without wind
    Disadvantages: No sails meant much crew labor was required; long, narrow design couldn't cope with heavy Atlantic seas

7. Nao
    Nation/people: Southern Europeans, especially Portugal and Spain
    Advantages: Lateen sail for traveling close to the wind; high castles (built-up ends) to withstand heavy seas; expanded cargo holds; sturdy
    Disadvantages: Less maneuverable and slower than the caravel

Navigation Aids

1. Astrolabe: Determine latitude (by measuring angle of the sun or stars)

2. Hourglass: Measure elapsed time when calculating a ship's speed, and also to count how many half-hour periods had elapsed while on a particular tack, or course

3. Cross staff: Determine latitude (by measuring altitude of the sun or stars)

4. Compass: Determine direction, via a magnetic needle

5. Quadrant: Determine latitude, again by measuring angles of heavenly bodies

6. Knot line and float: Determine ship's speed by measuring how long it took for the float to travel from bow to stern when thrown overboard, sometimes measured by knots in the float line

Extra Challenge: This could be a small-group project, with each group choosing one tool and giving a class presentation to explain how the tool works, including a live demonstration. (As an Extra Extra Challenge, ask interested students to demonstrate and explain the use of the traverse board.)

Columbus and the Ocean Sea

Part 1: The map doesn't show North and South America. This concept of the world meant that Columbus seriously underestimated the length of the voyage westward from Europe to Asia (even if it had been possible)—2,400 miles according to Columbus, but 11,000 in reality.

Part 2: Students should use the northeast winds to get to America from Spain, and the westerlies to get back, as Columbus did. The Viking route uses the northeast winds (in the northern area), then returns with the westerlies south of their outward voyage.

Christopher Columbus: In His Own Words

Students could take turns reading the log passages aloud in class.

What Columbus Tells Us

1. He persists in believing that Cuba is Japan.

2. He wants to convert the natives to Christianity, and he wants to find gold.

3. His "grand design" is to provide the monarchs of Spain with enough wealth to finance a war to take Jerusalem.

4. Perhaps to please these "heavenly" visitors, because Columbus clearly wants gold. Perhaps to get these strange visitors to leave their own islands. Perhaps they have a vague knowledge that the gold-rich Aztec society exists somewhere.

5. In Mexico, home of the Aztec.

6. He thinks they are gentle, friendly, simple, trusting, timid, and quick to learn (except for the Caribs, who are aggressive and threatening). He also thinks they will be easy to dominate and convert to Christianity.

7. He thinks the Spanish should convert the natives to Christianity and convert them to Spanish customs and ways of life. He thinks they should perform labor for the Spanish colonizers.

8. Europeans did go on to dominate, subjugate, and enslave native populations and attempt to wipe out native cultures.

Who Really Discovered America?

After all groups have made their presentations, you could lead a class discussion/debate about the probability/fact that any of these early discoveries actually occurred.

One useful source is *The Discovery of America* by Renardo Barden (San Diego: Greenhaven Press, 1989).

Why Explore?

Generally, the following categories apply to all the colonizing nations: *trade routes, acquire land, religion: spread it, check rival nation's power,* and *fortune.*

Religion: practice it freely came into play for later colonizers who sought freedom to practice Protestantism, or Catholicism, or sects of Protestantism persecuted by major denominations. Each nation had people in one of these categories. *Fame* and *adventure* were motives inspiring individual explorers and colonizers—for example, John Smith, Francisco Pizarro, and Vasco da Gama.

Additional Activity Suggestions

You could have students do any of the following additional activities.

1. Imagine you are a cabin boy or a sailor on one of Columbus's ships on the 1492 trip. Write a series of diary entries as the voyage goes on. What do you fear about the unknown seas you are sailing into? Will you be one of the crew who demands that Columbus turn back? With classmates you could also role-play crew members discussing the perils of the voyage and whether or not to demand that Columbus turn back.

2. Read Columbus's entire log of the 1492 voyage. A good source is *The Log of Christopher Columbus,* translated by Robert H. Fuson (Camden, Maine: International Marine Publishing, 1987).

3. Gather quotations from 1892 and 1992 about Columbus and his voyages. How have ideas about Columbus the man and the results of his actions changed over the years?

4. Here's a small-group or individual contest: Find the most uses of the name of Columbus in the United States that you

can—place names, street names, vehicle names, and so on.

5. Create a time line of significant world exploration landmarks of the 1400's, 1500's, and 1600's—plus the Viking voyages.
   (Teacher Note: Unit 6 has students create a combined time line. You could lead up to that activity by having students create time lines for Units 1 through 5.)

Assessment

1. Describe the lands and populations Columbus found in 1492 and how his arrival affected those people.

2. Describe the navigational tools and geographic knowledge that were available to Columbus. Why was he motivated to take his voyage to the west? Why did he feel capable of making such a voyage?

3. Explain the motives that spurred European nations to sponsor overseas voyages of exploration.

Unit 5: Spain and Portugal in the Americas

Spain Explores the Americas

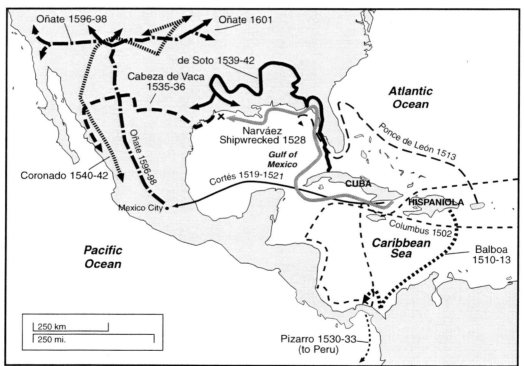

1. Columbus 1502
   Major accomplishment/failure:
   First European to land in Central America; failed to find passage to Indies; ended up stranded with crew on Jamaica for many months.

2. Balboa 1510–13
   Major accomplishment/failure:
   First European to view the Pacific Ocean.

3. Ponce de León 1513
   Major accomplishment/failure:

Found Florida and the Gulf Stream, but failed to find the Fountain of Youth.

4. Cortés 1519–21
   Major accomplishment/failure:
   Found and conquered the Aztec empire.

5. Narváez 1527–28
   Major accomplishment/failure:
   Was to settle Florida, but died in a shipwreck.

6. Pizarro 1530–33
   Major accomplishment/failure:
   Found and conquered the Inca empire.

7. Cabeza de Vaca 1535–36
   Major accomplishment/failure:

Survived years of subsistence slavery; explored areas of the U.S. Southwest.

8. de Soto 1539–42
   Major accomplishment/failure:
   Discovered Mississippi River, explored Southeast; alienated local Indians, died en route.

9. Coronado 1540–42
   Major accomplishment/failure:
   Spent years fruitlessly searching for the nonexistent Seven Cities of Cíbola, but did explore vast areas of present-day U.S. in the process.

10. Oñate 1596–98
    Major accomplishment/failure:
    First royal governor of New Mexico.

Mapping Mesoamerica

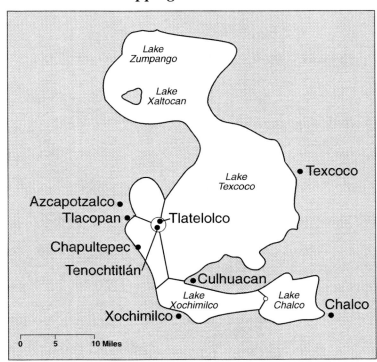

Questions:

1. It was hard to attack—could be approached only by causeways, via land.

2. It could be cut off by siege, which Cortés implemented.

3. Surrounding towns resented Aztec domination and conquest, so were happy to help Cortés defeat their enemy.

A Noble Society

Stratum 1

Emperor **(1a)**

Nobles **(1b)**

Rulers

Chiefs

Priests

Military leaders

Scribes

Stratum 2

Merchants

Fine artisans

Stratum 3

Commoners

Craft workers

Soldiers

Fishermen

Farmers

Stratum 4

Slaves

Extra Challenge

1. Spanish society was organized along similar lines, with an absolute monarch and a privileged nobility, merchants and fine artisans holding positions of special distinction, and commoners at the bottom of the heap, just above slaves. The two societies were similar, although Spanish conquistadors ruled as colonial powers. The Spanish system of rewarding conquistadors with land and people to work it was very much like the Aztec system of rewarding warriors.

2. The British and North American Indians were far apart in political and class structure. Also, in Spanish America intermarriage was common; many Indians assimilated the Christian god and saints into their traditional religious beliefs, so some religious bonds were formed between Spanish and Indians. Spanish colonial culture tended to be inclusive; British North America was quite different.

Inca, Aztec, or Maya?

This activity helps students note that these three cultures shared many similar characteristics.

1. Inca, Aztec, Maya

2. Aztec, Maya

3. Inca, Aztec, Maya

4. Maya, Aztec (Inca had no writing)

5. Inca, Aztec, Maya

6. Aztec, Maya

7. Inca, Aztec

8. Inca, Aztec (not much in Maya)

9. Inca, Aztec, Maya

10. Inca, Aztec (The Maya had frequent wars, but no empire. Instead, they had a number of kings and power centers.)

Why Come to Spanish America?

1. You come involuntarily, as a slave.

2. You want to convert Indians to Christianity, and you want to stop mistreatment of natives by the Spanish colonialists.

3. You are looking for adventure and riches.

4. Whether your husband wants you to join him or not, you go to Spanish America because the Spanish king has ordered that all men in the colonies with wives in Spain have to come back and get their spouses.

5. You are anxious to profit from the valuable trade between Spain and the colonial settlers.

6. Your older brother will inherit the family land and fortune, so you go to the Americas to gain your own fortune and lands.

7. You want to continue fighting—against non-Christians, and for the zest of fighting itself.

8. The Spanish king has ordered that you be sent to the colonies to become a wife for a Spanish settler.

Advising Cortés or Pizarro

1. Technology of war: Spanish had steel swords, crossbows, horses, gunpowder, muskets and cannon, steel shields. Indians had obsidian-bladed clubs, flint-tipped javelins, cotton armor, wooden shields.

2. Military strategy: Spanish fight to kill and conquer, Aztecs to capture warriors to use for human sacrifice.

3. Political problems within the Indian empire: Aztecs dominated other people in their empire by conquest and then demanded tribute from them; these people were happy to ally themselves with the Spanish to overthrow the Aztec rulers. The Incan empire was wracked by succession rivalries.

4. Disease: Natives of the Americas had no immunity to European diseases; many Indians would die, weakening any possible resistance to Spanish advances.

5. Role of religion: Spanish were partly motivated by the urge to spread Christianity, feeling their religion was the only true one, and needed by all peoples. Aztecs thought Cortés was their god Quetzalcoatl, coming back to take over the lands as he had promised, in the way predicted, so they gave in to the Spaniards more easily than they might otherwise have done. The Inca had a similar belief, which might have influenced the Inca ruler as well.

6. Use of trickery, treachery: In the Aztec empire, the ruler Montezuma welcomed Cortés as an honored guest, and Cortés then took Montezuma prisoner. In the Inca empire, Pizarro invited "the Inca" (the ruler) to meet with him, then attacked the unarmed entourage and took the Inca prisoner.

7. Role of terrain: For the Aztec conquest, Tenochtitlán was hard to get because of its island status and causeways, but easy to isolate because of the same factors. For the Inca conquest, Pizarro had to march through high-altitude mountainous country.

Slaves and Laborers

1. Children slaves: Yes
Property: Yes
Rights and freedoms: Few, if any

Property, freedom: No
Become slave: Captured by Africans, traded to Europeans

2. Land: Owned by the noble you must work for
Slave, property: No
Owe: Labor, services

3. Land: You, or your village, in common
Slave, property: No
Owe: Food, labor, tribute
Happen: You must work for your master involuntarily, as if you were a slave

4. Children slaves: No
Property: No (master owns only your labor, not yourself)
Rights, freedoms: Can marry, advance
Own property, buy freedom: Yes
Why slave: By gambling, poverty, criminal act; your parents or you yourself might have sold you into slavery

5. You are made a captive, branded, and distributed to the soldiers as a slave.

6. Land: Your clan or village group
Labor: You're a free laborer
Owe: Tribute

7. You must agree to accept the rule of the Catholic Church and the Spanish monarchs. Spanish soldiers can now make you and your family members slaves, take all you own, and even kill you.

The Spanish and the Indians: Two Views

1. The natives are peaceful, kind, and virtuous. The Spanish repay this with cruelty because all they want is wealth through gold.

2. The natives are uncultured, war-mongering pagans. It is the duty of civilized Christians to bring the benefits of Christian civilization to these people, by warfare and force as needed, and then to rule over them.

3. Priests, natives, and others who were distressed by the brutal and unfair Spanish policies and actions sided with Las Casas.

4. Those who profited by Spanish colonial policies and/or believed it was a duty and fine thing to spread Christianity sided with Sepúlveda.

Additional Activity Suggestions

You could have students do any of the following additional activities.

1. Read some of the original tales of the Spanish explorations. Cabeza de Vaca, for example, wrote about his adventures, and men who accompanied de Soto and Coronado also described their experiences.

2. See if you can find some Central or South American Indian descriptions of the Spanish conquerors written by those who experienced the events.

3. The Inca, Aztec, and Maya civilizations were impressive. Working individually or in groups, research one of these societies. Use what you learn to produce an interesting display that educates classmates about these people and their lives.

4. Figure out the Mayan mathematics system and demonstrate it to classmates.

5. Tell dramatically about the disturbing omens the Aztec experienced in the year before Cortés arrived. You could act out a discussion among Aztec priests or others who have gathered information about these omens.

Assessment

1. Compare the *encomienda* system with medieval European feudalism.

2. Explain why a relatively few Spanish conquistadors were able to overthrow the mighty Inca and Aztec empires.

Unit 6: Some Conclusions

The Columbian Exchange

Animals

Horses, cows, pigs, sheep, goats, chickens: Europe to the Americas

Turkeys, parrots: Americas to Europe

Human-made items

Guns, etc., metal tools: Europe to Americas and Africa

Hammocks: America to Europe

Precious metal crafts: America and Africa to Europe

Wheel: Europe to America

Food products

Potatoes, onions, radishes, lettuce, tobacco, maize, melons: Americas to Europe and Africa

Sugarcane, cane sugar: Europe to Americas

Bananas, coffee: Africa (via Asia) to Americas

Wheat, etc.: Europe to America

Ideas

Geography: Europe to Americas and Americas to Europe

Democracy: Americas to Europe

Democracy developed in colonial North America among British colonists, starting immediately (the Mayflower Compact), as British colonists instituted self-government, elections of officials, town assemblies, and so forth. This type of governing form was unknown in Europe. Native American societies in North America also were democratic. The British settlers' model eventually crossed the Atlantic to transform European monarchical governing forms.

What They Discovered

Answers will vary. Share and compare group or individual lists. Check to see that responses are on student maps.

Reading the "Human Cost" Graphs

1. 500,000   26,000   0

2. 11 million to 2.5 million; 8.5 million fewer; 4.5 million

3. two thirds

4. Mexico

5. Columbus arrived

6. Cortés arrived

7. No; natives died from a European-disease epidemic from earlier contact with white people.

The Age of Exploration Changes Europe

You could photocopy this page, mount the individual framed topics on a stiff backing, cut them out, and have students select topics from a "grab bag." Or you could assign topics as appropriate for particular groups or individual students.

Brief statements of the changes:

Knowledge of geography: New continents were discovered. The true extent of the "Ocean Sea" became known—and that it was two seas, the Atlantic and the Pacific. Geography became focused on observation, not on speculation.

What people ate and drank: The potato became a staple food of the European lower classes in northern countries and made it possible for populations to increase greatly. Coffee, tea, and sugar became extremely popular, fueling overseas trade.

Religious thought: The grip of dogma and the focus on narrowly interpreted Church law loosened. Natives of Africa and America demonstrated the possibility of worshiping a greater outside power that was not, strictly speaking, the Christian God.

Patterns of European political power: Nations that benefited economically from overseas trade and exploration gained power at the expense of others. Colonial powers became great rivals.

Ideas about government: Many native societies existed peacefully without kings, empires, codified laws, or private property; perhaps European governments could stand some change.

Medieval thought patterns: Acceptance of dogma, preconceptions, myth, and legend yielded to growing emphasis on acquiring knowledge through reason and fact.

European economy: Was transformed into a global, trade-dependent economy. Manufacturing grew in response to insatiable colonial demand for finished goods. Bankers and merchants became wealthy and powerful. The middle class expanded greatly; wealth and/or a good standard of living became accessible to many.

European nationalism: National self-pride and self-awareness grew in nations that became colonial powers.

Approaches to science: Science became discovery-based; conclusions were reached based on fact and observation rather than theory.

Combined Time Line

This would be an excellent group activity.

Assessment

The Age of Exploration Changes Europe and the Combined Time Line are both excellent assessment vehicles.

ADDITIONAL RESOURCES

Historical Fiction for Students

Baker, Betty. *Walk the World's Rim* (Cabeza de Vaca).

O'Dell, Scott. (novels about Spanish *conquistadors* in the Americas) *The King's Fifth* trilogy: *The Captive, The Feathered Serpent, The Amethyst Ring*

Wojciechowska, Maia. *Odyssey of Courage: The Story of Alvar Nuñez Cabeza de Vaca.*

Nonfiction for Students

Primary Sources

The Log of Christopher Columbus (various versions)

Narratives of: Alvar Nuñez Cabeza de Vaca, the De Soto expedition, and the Coronado expedition (various versions)

Reference Books

Brenner, Barbara. *If You Were There in 1492.*

Erdoes, Richard, and Alfonso Ortiz, eds. *American Indian Myths and Legends.*

Faber, Harold. *The Discoverers of America.*

Fritz, Jean. *Brendan the Navigator: A History Mystery About the Discovery of America.*

_____. *Where Do You Think You're Going, Christopher Columbus?*

Hargrove, Jim. *Ferdinand Magellan.*

Legay, Gilbert. *Atlas of Indians of North America.*

McKissack, Patricia and Frederick. *The Royal Kingdoms of Ghana, Mali and Songhay: Life in Medieval Africa.*

Monroe, Jean Guard, and Ray A. Williamson. *First Houses: Native American Homes and Sacred Structures.*

Sattler, Helen Roney. *The Earliest Americans.*

Syme, Ronald. *De Soto, Finder of the Mississippi.*

Collections of Primary Source Documents: Print

The Annals of America, Vol. 1. Chicago: Encyclopedia Britannica, 1968.

Commager, Henry Steele, ed. *Documents of American History,* 9th ed. (2 vols.). Englewood Cliffs, NJ: Prentice-Hall, 1973.

Craven, Avery, Walter Johnson, and F. Roger Dunn. *A Documentary History of the American People.* Boston: Ginn and Company, 1951.

Hart, Albert Bushnell. *American History as Told by Contemporaries* (5 volumes). New York: The Macmillan Company, 1901.

Historical Abstracts of the United States. Washington, DC: U.S. Department of Commerce, Bureau of the Census, 1975.

MacDonald, William, ed. *Select Charters and Other Documents Illustrative of American History 1606–1775.* New York: The Macmillan Company, 1899.

CD-ROM

America Adventure. Knowledge Adventure (also available as a DOS floppy disk).

American Indian 2.0. Facts On File.

American Journey—History in Your Hands: Women in America. Research Publications.

CD Sourcebook of American History. InfoBases.

500 Nations. Microsoft.

Landmark Documents in American History. Facts on File (dwarfs the print collections).

World Wide Web/Internet

Sites with Numerous Links to U.S. History Sources:

Government/Social Studies Sources (includes listings of Library of Congress exhibits, historical documents from Project Gutenburg, other social studies Web sites): http://www.nwoca.ohio.gov/www/gov.html

History/Social Studies Web Site for K–12 Teachers (includes site map, What's New Archive, sources arranged by category): http://www.execpc.com/˜dboals/boals.html

Library of Congress home page (includes American Memory historical collections): http://lcweb.loc.gov

Kathy Schrock's site (a Cape Cod teacher's excellent list of resources): http://www.capecod.net/schrockguide

U.S. Historic Documents (primary documents in full text): http://www.ukans.edu/carrie/docs/amdocs_index.html

GLOSSARY

Age of Exploration—the years from the late 1400's to the 1600's when Europeans sailed to parts of the world they had never been to before.

archaeology—the scientific study of the physical remains of past human life and activities.

Beringia—the land bridge that existed between today's Siberia and Alaska during the most recent Ice Age, 30,000 to 14,000 years ago.

caravan—a group of travelers going on a journey through a desert or other difficult terrain; also, a train of pack animals carrying cargo.

Columbian exchange—the exchange of cultural and natural items among Europeans, Native Americans, and Africans when these peoples began to intermingle after Columbus's voyage to the Americas.

conquistador—a leader in the Spanish conquest of the Inca and Aztec empires in the Americas.

Crusades—military expeditions launched by Christians in the eleventh, twelfth, and thirteenth centuries to take back Christian holy places in the Middle East from Muslims.

cultural trait—a type of behavior or belief that is customary to a particular human group.

currency—something used like money to exchange goods.

deity—supreme being, god, goddess.

ethnic—relating to races or large groups of people tied together by common customs and traits.

fuedalism—political system in Europe from the ninth to the fifteenth centuries based on ruling lords, nobles who served them, and landless tenants called serfs, who were bound to work the land and work for the lords.

Ice Age—a time in prehistory when areas of the world were covered by enormous bodies of ice called glaciers.

Islam—the Muslim religion, founded by Mohammed in 610.

kinship—being related; state of being part of a group of people of common ancestry.

Mesoamerica—the region of Central America where Aztec, Maya, and other native societies flourished before the coming of the Europeans.

migrate—to move from one country or place to another; a **migrant** is a person who migrates.

Muslim—follower of Islam, the religion founded by Mohammed in 610.

navigation—the method of getting ships from place to place.

nomadic—roaming from place to place, usually seasonally, to secure a group's food supply.

pilgrimage—a trip to a sacred religious place by a religious worshiper.

strata—layers or levels.

terrain—physical features of land; also an area or region.

transatlantic—crossing the Atlantic Ocean.

J. WESTON WALCH PUBLISHER

Share Your Bright Ideas with Us!

We want to hear from you! Your valuable comments and suggestions will help us meet your current and future classroom needs.

Your name_____Date_____

School name_____Phone_____

School address_____

Grade level taught_____Subject area(s) taught_____Average class size_____

Where did you purchase this publication?_____

Was your salesperson knowledgeable about this product?   Yes_____   No_____

What monies were used to purchase this product?

____School supplemental budget   ____Federal/state funding   ____Personal

Please "grade" this Walch publication according to the following criteria:

	A	B	C	D	F
Quality of service you received when purchasing	A	B	C	D	F
Ease of use	A	B	C	D	F
Quality of content	A	B	C	D	F
Page layout	A	B	C	D	F
Organization of material	A	B	C	D	F
Suitability for grade level	A	B	C	D	F
Instructional value	A	B	C	D	F

COMMENTS:_____

_____

What specific supplemental materials would help you meet your current—or future—instructional needs?

_____

Have you used other Walch publications? If so, which ones?_____

May we use your comments in upcoming communications?   ____Yes   ____No

Please **FAX** this completed form to **207-772-3105**, or mail it to:

Product Development, J. Weston Walch, Publisher, P.O. Box 658, Portland, ME 04104-0658

We will send you a **FREE GIFT** as our way of thanking you for your feedback. **THANK YOU!**